LAO TZU ೞ TAO TE CHING

KEITH SEDDON

The *Tao Te Ching* is the principle classic of ancient Chinese Taoism. It was written over 2000 years ago, but its wisdom is timeless. From Tao all things come, and to it all things return. Find contentment by embracing the Tao, by curbing desire, and by pursuing simplicity.

This clear new translation is accompanied by an Introduction that explains the philosophy of Lao Tzu's Taoism, and by a Glossary that explains key concepts.

Keith Seddon is a freelance academic and author. He is Professor of Philosophy at Warnborough College Ireland.

Lao Tzu

Tao Te Ching

A New Version, with Introduction, Notes, Glossary and Index

Keith Seddon

Lulu

Hardback edition first published 2008
by Keith Seddon
at Lulu
www.lulu.com

First published in paperback 2006
by Lulu
www.lulu.com

ISBN 978–0–955–68443–2 (hardback)
ISBN 978–1–847–28263–7 (paperback)

Even though my words are easy to
    understand and easy to put into practice,
No one in the world really knows them or
    lives by them.

Lao Tzu, *Tao Te Ching*, Chapter 70

畫松法

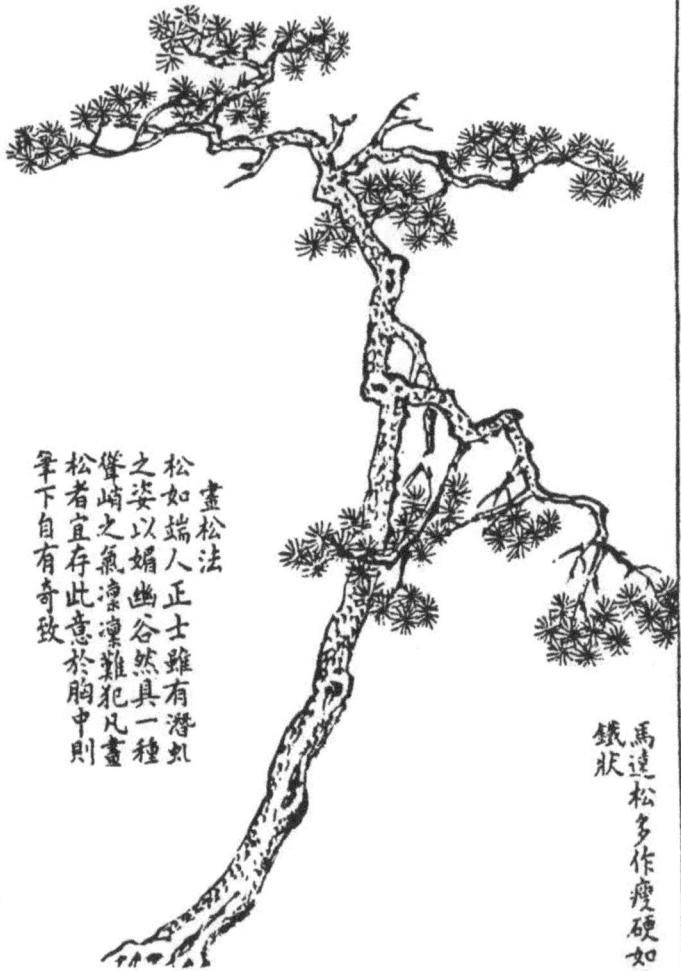

松如端人正士雖有潛虬
之姿以媚幽谷然具一種
聳峭之氣凜凜難犯凡畫
松者宜存此意於胸中則
筆下自有奇致

馬遠松多作瘦硬如屈
鐵狀

CONTENTS

INTRODUCTION

In making this version of the *Tao Te Ching* my motive has been to extend to others the outlook that this ancient text cultivated in me throughout fifteen years of study. We live today in a profoundly materialistic society in which a person's worth is measured almost exclusively by their job, status and their capacity to consume. The potential for developing our spiritual natures is swamped at every turn by the insistent siren call of consumerism and by the frantic demands of a society that has no sense of its own direction. But as the *Tao Te Ching* teaches, once an extreme has been reached it cannot endure and, inevitably, trends are invoked which begin to reverse the situation. Thus, as we move into the new millennium we see the 'new age' begin to flourish. Some people at least realise that it does matter how we treat our own minds and bodies, and how we treat the environment. As we see the effects of pollution and the damage done to the natural world we also see that the old ways must be changed or else abandoned.

The compilers of the *Tao Te Ching*, writing over two thousand years ago in China, had a similar vision. They lived at a time when the pursuit of wealth, status and political power plunged the country into repeated civil wars as one after another petty little states fought against their neighbours vying for power. (Historians quickly came to refer to these times as the Warring States Period.) For some generations, life for ordinary people was precarious and unpleasant. The *Tao Te Ching*, ostensibly written for the ruler to help him perform his role responsibly, reveals a path to a more harmonious way of life, both for society as a whole if only the ruler (and by implication the government as a whole) would embrace its precepts, *and* for the isolated individual who is prepared to give up the trivial squabbling for status and wealth.

THE SPIRITUAL PATH

This path towards a more harmonious way of life is taken by adopting a new spiritual perspective, of coming to realise where the sacred can be found, and of finding what has true value and is worth pursuing. By embracing the Tao, we can each of us come to find this new spiritual perspective, in which personal ambitions and desires for material goods diminishes to the point of disappearing, and from where we find that pursuing simplicity and giving up things results in tranquillity and peace of mind. And from this perspective we see that disaster awaits if we try to interfere with the natural order of things; a better way is to trust that the mysterious Tao will produce from within itself a world that is in fact the best, a world that is best left alone, and a world to which we find we can attach ourselves with joy. After all, what is the alternative? The alternative is to stay as we are, pretty much dissatisfied with things, forever interfering with things in an effort to make them go better, rarely accepting what is just 'all right', but insisting on 'more and better'.

Once we have enjoyed the perspective that embracing the Tao can bring, it is hard to give it up. To be sure, we may stumble sometimes and get confused. But hopefully, most of us will find the Tao again, perhaps to the degree that talk of finding the Tao becomes superfluous, because we are in it all the time, as were the Taoist sages of ancient times.

TAO

It hardly needs to be stated, but obviously the key to understanding the wisdom of the *Tao Te Ching* is to find a way to understand the concept of the Tao itself. 'Tao' is a Chinese expression that literally means 'way', or 'path'. Many translations of Taoist texts, including the *Tao Te Ching* and books about Taoism, leave the term untranslated, as I shall do in this book. Some translators and commentators decide to translate 'Tao' as 'Way'. Tao can be the way that something is done, and the path that one follows to a destination. In the sense of the 'way that things are done', in Confucian texts,

'Tao' is used to mean 'human behaviour', and 'moral law' – that is, the 'Way of Man'. In contrast to this, the *Tao Te Ching* and other Taoist texts employ 'Tao' in a new sense, a metaphysical sense, to identify that which underpins, gives rise to, and sustains all things in the universe. Thus, in Taoist thought, the Tao is what brings things into existence, what sustains them, and what they return to when they cease to exist.

Taoists maintain that the Tao is quite literally beyond our grasp. Thus we find in the *Tao Te Ching* such lines as:

> Looked for, it cannot be seen: it is not visible (14a).

> It is called the formless form and the imageless
> image.
> That is why it is called obscure and indistinct (14b).

> Tao is invisible and intangible (21a).

Whatever its true nature really might be, it is actually *nothing*, not made of anything, not composed of substance. The only things that we can grasp, in the sense of getting our hands around and lifting them up, are physical *things*. The *Tao Te Ching* is quite insistent that the Tao is not a thing. It 'gives rise' to things (51a), somehow or other it *makes* them, but is itself not a thing. *Forms* are made by physical substances being arranged in various ways. Getting to grips with physical substances and their forms – quite literally – occupies the young human mind for several years. The things that physical substance can be made into, either naturally (pebbles, trees, horses, etc.) or by manufacture (tables, chairs, books, etc.) are extremely numerous and almost infinite in their variety. That this is the world we find ourselves living in – a world stuffed with stuff formed into things – we take entirely for granted. If we try to imagine a different sort of world, we tend to imagine a place filled with just different sorts of things: in our fantasy world, these things might take different forms, and might change in a variety of different ways, but the fantasy works because we inject into it our idea of substance and things. A world without substance and things cannot be imagined.

But why should the world be here at all? And why should the things in it be as they are, possessed of the properties they just happen to have?

The Taoists say that the *Tao made it all*. Not only does the Tao bring things into being, it also sustains them through every moment, making them change in the way they do, until eventually they fall apart, get eaten, get burned up or what have you, such that they 'return to the source' – that is, they go back to where they came from: nothingness. Whatever you are sitting on as you read this, Tao brought it into being, through natural processes, or through all those processes required to make a manufactured object. The reason why it just doesn't vanish in the next second is because Tao sustains it – keeps it going as it were, keeps 'pushing it out' into the world of things. And the reason why it will eventually decay and disintegrate is because this is Tao's way. If everything lasted forever just as it is, there would be no room for any changes, no room for anything to happen; and no room for us to do all the odd, mysterious, delightful, violent, caring, thoughtless and thoughtful things that people do!

For of course, we are ourselves only different sorts of things. No doubt we often think of ourselves as 'better', 'more sophisticated' and of course 'more important' than 'mere' things. Even if we are special things, we are things nevertheless, and we are as we are because the Tao brought us into being and sustains us just as we find ourselves.

How the Tao makes the world, and *why* it makes it, are deeply mysterious questions that simply cannot be answered. The world's being here, in the way that it happens to be, is a complete mystery. But the Taoist doesn't declare 'I wish I could solve this mystery! This mystery troubles me!' No: the Taoist declares that this is a *wonderful mystery*. It's a mystery worth having. Indeed, the Taoists 'embrace' this mystery, in the sense that they 'embrace the Tao'. And doing that makes all the difference – absolutely *all the difference* – as to how one regards oneself and one's engaging in the world.

THE TAO CANNOT BE NAMED

The *Tao Te Ching* tells us that the Tao is so mysterious that it is not possible to tell anyone about it, because it is not possible to explain it in words:

> The Tao that can be put in words is not the ever-abiding Tao (1a).

To attempt to explain it would be to delimit and sketch out merely a sort of Tao. Certainly, something would be said, but not enough to capture all that is true of the Tao.

We have to accept that no explanation of the Tao can be complete. Whatever we say, more is left out than is put in: however *much* we say, we will never have said enough. But this doesn't mean that what little we *do* say is entirely worthless.

The Tao 'cannot be told' because it is beyond our capacity to correctly and fully conceptualise it. To say that 'the Tao that can be put in words is not the ever-abiding Tao', is to say the same thing. Even to name it 'Tao' means that we have in the attempt failed to name it.

This will be clearer if we consider how naming works in the more usual context of naming people and things. When we use an ordinary proper name we pick someone out, pull him or her into the foreground as it were and push everything else into the background. Thus they stand exposed against this background and in the spotlight of their name, so to speak. They are illuminated for all to see. Thus 'Peter' picks out a unique individual. *He* is the one we mean, and all the others we *don't* mean. He is who he is in virtue of his unique characteristics, *and* in *not* having any of the characteristics he lacks. In short, in the act of naming, we perform the intellectual task of pulling something forward in our attention for scrutiny, exposing or contrasting it against *everything else there is*.

Essentially the same thing is done when we use ordinary nouns, like 'tree', or 'horse', or 'book'. We can refer to horses as a complete set, meaning to include for scrutiny all horses alive today, or perhaps all horses that have ever lived and

will ever live. If we say 'horses are good at running' we mean
to pick out all horses. And we pick them out to contrast them
against everything else there is. Even though greyhounds are
also good at running, it's *horses* we mean to discuss. To pick
out an individual horse, we say 'this horse', or 'that horse',
and when we say that, we mean to pull forward that one
creature for scrutiny.

If we couldn't say this, if we couldn't pick out sets and
individuals using names and nouns, we wouldn't be able to
say anything about anything. For that is the point of naming.
Having 'hooked' something with a name ('Peter' or 'that
horse', for example) we can now say something about them:
we might say 'Peter embraces the Tao' or 'that horse is as fast
as the wind'. And for human beings, living the sorts of lives
that we do, saying things about things is extremely important.

Indeed, with our capacity to name things we do more
than just say things about things – we also ask questions,
issue commands, tell jokes, coax people, offer bribes, make
promises, and so on. Without the capacity to name things,
civilisation could never have got started.

The Taoist says that the Tao cannot be named because the
Tao is not that sort of thing (it is not a thing) that can be
pulled forward and set in contrast against a background of
everything else. The Tao is not *in the world,* so cannot be
pulled forward and contrasted against everything else in the
world as the horse can. Even to say, 'Well, here on one hand
is the world, and here on the other hand is the Tao,' fails to
pull the Tao forward in the sense that we have 'hooked' it
with its name. There isn't anything there to scrutinise, nothing against which it stands out. It has no properties it can
stand out *with.*

And most importantly for Taoists, to name something is to
delimit it. That's what being 'picked out' means: it means to
draw the limit around something – or in the case of the
horses, to draw a boundary around just *those* types of creature. To name something both says what it is (horse: hairy,
four legs, runs fast) *and* to say what it is not (horse: not gase-
ous, not made of jam, not living on Venus).

Because the Tao is not *in* the world, but is thought of as that which gives rise *to* the world, anything we say about it must be somehow or other inadequate. The language we use is for use *in* the world: though even in the world, we must be careful – tomatoes are red, but electricity is not, or rather electricity cannot be discussed in terms of colour. And the language we use *in* the world is entirely inappropriate for discussing the Tao.

This is why the *Tao Te Ching* talks about the Tao in negative terms, because quite simply, the terms do not apply. Thus the Tao has no form, makes no sound, cannot be imagined, has no name, and in calling it 'Tao', we are merely attempting to name that which cannot be named.

THE TAO IS MYSTERIOUS

How strange, how bizarre, that there should be this Something that is not a Thing behind the world and all the things in the world. It pushes everything out into the world and makes everything substantial. It sustains everything from moment to moment so that nothing is forgotten, nothing just slips out of existence. Through its actions, everything *is*, and we *are*. And we are such that we can look at everything that Is and wonder why, and how, it all should be.

So, there is a Something that is not a Thing – we will call it 'Tao' – that sustains all things. What can we say of the Tao? Alas, very little. It is not the sort of thing that our speech or our thoughts can capture. It is deeply mysterious. We cannot see it, we cannot hear it, and we cannot grasp it. It has no form. Yet from it, all forms derive their being.

Could we say that it exists? No, it doesn't even exist, because it is not that sort of thing that might exist or might not exist. Only things in the world might exist or might not exist. To find out whether there is a piano in my back room, we can go to look. And lo! There it is! There against that wall *is* a piano. But there is nowhere we can look for the Tao. It neither exists nor does not exist.

The theologians are fond of proving God's existence. They spend their time – or certainly some of them have done –

concocting clever arguments and picking apart the arguments of their rivals. The Taoist is not so silly. The Tao's existence cannot be proved, and it cannot be disproved. It neither exists nor does not exist. It is there is some sense, and what this sense is can be alluded to vaguely, and that is all. It is there in the sense that it originates everything and sustains everything. But the How and the Why of this cannot be answered.

But here is a clue to the Taoist's outlook. Don't look too deeply. Wisdom is found not in the complicated and the profound, but in the plain and ordinary. Taoists find their contentment, their inner harmony, their way of life, in following Nature. Nature is so, because the Tao makes it so. In following Nature, one is following Tao.

THE TAO NEVER ACTS

'The Tao never acts, yet nothing is left undone' (37a). *Wu wei* is one of the major concepts employed by the *Tao Te Ching*. *Wu wei* is variously translated as 'non-action', 'non-active', 'does nothing', and 'never acts'. *Wu* means 'without', and *wei* means 'work' or 'doing' or 'acting'.

Just as the Tao is *wu ming*, without name, the Tao is also *wu wei*, 'without action'. The Tao cannot be named, because there is no background against which it can be contrasted by the act of naming, and in attempting to name it, we would inadequately be attempting to delimit it – when the Tao is not a thing that has limits. Similarly it is impossible for us to say *how* the Tao does what it does – make the world, and sustain it – and impossible for us even to entertain the idea that the Tao actually *does* anything. Things *in* the world act and do things all the time. It is difficult for us to stop them from doing things. It is the nature of things to do things. Things interact with other things, causing this, and causing that, in a never-ending unfolding of events. Things happen: things change. This is the nature of the world.

But the Tao is not *in* the world, and it would be wrong to attempt to describe it in the terms we use of *things in the world*. Our notion of 'act' or 'work' is always applied against a background of what is already there and what is already happening. Thus, we act to change something from how it would otherwise be to how *we* want it to be. In acting, we *intervene* in the natural course of events, and make something *different* happen.

But the Tao makes everything. Whatever it is the Tao does, its doing this brings about the whole world. How can the Tao act to make things different from how they would otherwise be? *However* they are, the Tao makes them so. The Tao cannot actually change anything.

Change is what you get when one thing causes an effect in something else. The match igniting the gas, the wind blowing down a slate, the hammer in the piano striking the string, are all clear examples of cause and effect. But the Tao does not act by causing effects. The Tao does not act by causing a wind and seeing what will happen. The Tao brings into being, pushes out into existence, *the whole shebang*. The Tao brings into being the entire background against which it is *possible* for a high wind to dislodge a slate. The Tao brings into being absolutely everything that was, that is, and that which is to come. To say that the Tao might *act* to do this one thing *here*, is clearly ridiculous.

The Taoist, in declaring that the Tao is *wu wei* is also pointing, again, to the deeply mysterious nature of the Tao. Clearly *something* is happening: the world is coming about. At every moment it *keeps on* coming about. That this is so, and what is behind it all, is deeply mysterious. What is merely mysterious, we might one day fathom and understand. But the Taoist says that the Tao, its nature, and the world's coming about are *deeply mysterious* – that is, forever *beyond understanding*.

Some people call this 'mystical', which is as good a term as any. But from accepting what is mystical, comes a perspective on the practical affairs of everyday life.

> In pursuit of knowledge, something new is learned every day.
> In pursuit of the Tao, something is abandoned every day.

> Do less and less
> Until non-action is achieved.
> Do nothing, and nothing remains undone.
>
> All things can be accomplished by not acting.
> The empire can never be governed by taking action
>   (48).

The Taoist takes the Tao, and the natural world brought into being by the Tao, as models for their own conduct. To say that the way to get things done is through not acting, is at best a puzzle, and at worst a nonsense. The original writers or compilers of the *Tao Te Ching* clearly had a taste for the paradoxical saying. But we should remind ourselves that stating a seeming paradox is just one way in which an aphorism can make its impact.

The *Tao Te Ching* is not advocating that, in the practical sphere of daily life, we should literally take no action. We cannot live at all without acting to sustain ourselves with food and drink. The Taoist makes a distinction between natural and spontaneous action that reacts to circumstances as they arise, and action that is motivated by desires for particular ends (especially wealth and status). The follower of Tao takes the Tao as a model by not interfering in the natural flow of events; such a person *takes part* in the unfolding of events, but does not *intervene* to consciously *change* events. To do this is to stand back as it were and let things take their own course, in accord with their own natures.

To do this, the Taoist believes, is better for the world at large, and better for the individual.

CONTENTMENT

> There is no crime greater than having desires.
> No disaster is greater than not being content with
>   one's lot.
> The worst misfortune is to be greedy.
> He who is content with what he has
> Has enough (46b).

We cannot be content if we are envious of others and want what they have. Not being content, says the *Tao Te Ching*, is a disaster. It is a disaster in more than one sense. Someone who is not content will be agitated, upset, frustrated, annoyed – certainly they will be far from the tranquillity that the Taoist values, and to this extent their lack of contentment is a disaster. But it is a disaster also in the sense that – hardly surprisingly – the discontented person will take action to remedy their misery. They will respond to their desires and take action to satisfy them. As often as not, in today's society, this will amount to someone doing something as seemingly innocuous as going for a promotion at work because they want to get a bigger salary than their neighbour, or because they want to buy the latest TV or wonder-gizmo for the kitchen or workshop.

We must admit, to one extent or another, we all do it.

But why does the *Tao Te Ching* call this a *crime*?

Some people will appreciate this sentiment more easily than others will. Some will find the following analysis pretty straightforward and obvious, whilst others will be hostile to it. For those in the latter group, I am tempted to ask you not to *react* to my account, but to put aside your initial reaction and instead take some time to consider, over days and weeks if necessary, the points being made.

Having too many desires leads to exactly the sort of society we have ended up with today. From all sides we are bombarded by advertisements and other enticements urging us to buy this, acquire that, do this, go there. Magazine articles show us what we have not got, but what we should have. We are repeatedly shown images of the ideal room, the ideal house, the better car, the better holiday, and of course, the perfect body, complete with perfect hair. The message is clear: if we had these things, or even a proportion of them, we would be content; in some sense or other, we would be happy.

These advertisements and articles have their effect by undermining any contentment we might happen to be enjoying. If we were already satisfied with what we have, manufacturers and retailers would sell a mere fraction of what they currently sell. An advertisement trying to get us to buy Product X works by attempting to show that in *having* it, we will be happy, or at least happier than we would be without it, as well as conjuring in us a sense of discontent and perhaps inadequacy for *not having* it.

Acquiring material goods, to be sure, can serve as a sort of distraction from our overall level of contentment, our being always in the presence of one desire or another for this, or for that. Yet acquiring material goods cannot in itself lead to personal fulfilment and well-being.

Notice how deep-rooted acquisitiveness is in our society. The person who has resisted its clutches is at best thought odd, and at worst is ridiculed. To stand apart from the general herd and do without any number of the latest fads establishes one as an eccentric who is suspect simply because they find value in other things. Driven by desires kindled by the ideals of mass-consumerism, we work longer and longer hours, damaging our health, spending too little time with our children and, oddly, spending little time with our new acquisitions. Or in the case of acquiring a new car, probably spending *too much* time in it, stuck in traffic day after day because *everyone* wants a car, and *everyone* wants to live somewhere nice, miles away from where they want to work and shop.

Some have dubbed this the 'rat race'; and you can see why. There is no *direction* to the race; there is no *finish* to it. Everyone is madly careering about, and no one has much of an idea why he or she or anybody else is doing it.

And after decades of consumerism it is quite apparent what is written on the bottom line: the degradation and destruction of the natural environment. Where it will end, no one knows. But to make our society take a different route, all we can do is change *our own* outlooks. We should try to distinguish what we really *need* from what the advertisements tell us we merely *want*. We should decide that contentment and happiness do not describe a place we *will* get to (after that promotion, when I have a new car, when I have X and Y and Z) but describe a state of mind, an outlook, a way of being in the world in which contentment is with us *right now, right here.*

To work on our own outlooks, and to do this as Taoists, following the teachings of the *Tao Te Ching*, we should start with simplicity. If we can make just a bit of progress here, and if we can begin to have a sense of the mysterious Tao moment by moment bringing everything about, the rest will begin to fall into place. We will find that we can more easily give up what we don't need, and also perhaps find that we need less than we thought we did. We will begin to relax our grip a bit and let events take their course; we will suggest instead of order; we will encourage instead of compel; we will abandon competing and find tranquillity. And we will calmly accept what the Tao brings us; we will travel on the road (*tao*) of life with fewer hopes and expectations, and we will stumble into fewer anxieties and disappointments. We will find what it means to 'embrace the Tao' in our own personal way, and we will communicate the wonderment of our spiritual path by the example of our lives, and like the Sage of the *Tao Te Ching* we will lead without being at the front. We will live in Tao and embrace the mystery.

AUTHORSHIP AND ORIGIN OF THE *TAO TE CHING*

It seems readily apparent that the wisdom and insights that one can glean by reading the *Tao Te Ching* can be appreciated quite independently from any knowledge that one may have of the work's author and origin. All the same, it is quite natural to wish to satisfy one's curiosity as to who wrote the *Tao Te Ching* and the circumstances that gave rise to its creation.

There is just one source which modern scholarship can cite which offers a biography of Lao Tzu. This is the *Shih Chi* (*Historical Records*), which provides the first general history of China from the earliest times to the reign of Wu–ti (140–87 BC). It was begun by Ssu-ma T'an who died in 110 BC, and completed by his son, Ssu-ma Ch'ien (145–*c*.86 BC). This book tells us that Lao Tzu was an older contemporary of Confucius (551–479 BC). Having lived for a long time in the state of Chou (where he had risen to the post of court archivist), he became despondent at seeing the society slip further and further into moral decline, and he decided to leave. When he got to the pass at Han Ku[1] which led out of the country, the Keeper of the Pass, Kuan Yin[2] said to Lao Tzu, 'Since you are about to leave the world, can you write a book?' Lao Tzu obliged by writing the *Tao Te Ching*, after which he went on his way. Nobody knows what happened to him after this.

The *Shih Chi* also records that Confucius went to Chou to ask Lao Tzu about ceremonial rites, but doesn't say anything about what was actually said about rites. Instead, it contains a lecture that Lao Tzu gave on the sort of behaviour that should be avoided.

Ssu-ma T'an and his son probably drew on several sources to get this account. Many of their possible sources of course no longer survive, but some do. We find in the *Chuang Tzu*[3] (fourth century BC) an account of the meeting between Confucius and Lao Tzu, at which Lao Tzu criticises certain aspects of Confucian thought (but doesn't say anything about rites), and in the *Li Chi* (*Record of Rites*: first century BC) there are four instances of Confucius explaining what he learned about rites from Lao Tzu, but there is no mention of the meeting itself.

Reliable details about the life of the man who wrote the *Tao Te Ching* (if indeed this work was written by just a single author) will probably never be known. The name 'Lao Tzu' tells us next to nothing. 'Tzu' is not really a name at all. It appears in the names of many Chinese philosophers and is just a courteous appellation meaning 'master' in the sense of 'teacher'.[4] 'Lao' simply means 'old'. (Old age was revered as a sign of great wisdom.) Thus 'Lao Tzu' means 'old master'. If this was indeed ever the name of someone who really existed, it cannot have been his real name, but was a sort of professional *nom de plume*, and may well have been coined by his followers. On the other hand, 'Lao Tzu' may have been invented as a name under which teachers and students could put any number of disparate and diverse philosophical ideas and sayings. It is certainly not impossible to imagine that as time went by this miscellany took on more and more of what would later be recognised as having a distinctly Taoist flavour. Perhaps at some point an editor, or series of editors, sorted through this material and produced the text of what became known as the *Tao Te Ching*.

The book attributed to Mencius (372?–289? BC), a Confucian philosopher, makes no mention of Lao Tzu or the teaching contained in the *Tao Te Ching*. It does, however, discuss other schools, and this omission indicates that the *Tao Te Ching* was compiled after the time of Mencius, and does not after all (despite what the *Shih Chi* says about Lao Tzu) date from the sixth century BC.[5]

This hypothesis is supported by the fact that the *Chuang Tzu* book (contemporary with the *Mencius*) similarly makes no mention of Lao Tzu's school of Taoism, yet it does refer to three other schools which by this time had gained a reputation for themselves: the Confucian school (founded two hundred years before the writing of the *Chuang Tzu*), the school of Mo Tzu (founded shortly after the death of Confucius), and the school of Yang Chu (founded in the fourth century BC). There being no mention of Lao Tzu's school of Taoism implies one of two things: either Chuang Tzu was indeed unaware of Lao Tzu's thought (indicating that Lao Tzu should be placed some time after Chuang Tzu) or that perhaps Lao Tzu's school, already in existence at this time, had yet to acquire any prominence.[6] Neither of these suppositions is consistent with the *Tao Te Ching* dating from the sixth century BC.[7]

If we look more closely into the alleged meeting between Confucius and Lao Tzu by analysing other texts from this period, we find that the story of the meeting was not widely known until the second half of the third century BC. In all probability, the story originated at this time, and cannot be relied upon as fact.

The style that the *Tao Te Ching* is written in tells its own story. Before Confucius it is fair to assume that no one was writing in a private, non-official capacity: no such works are known, and none are referred to. Therefore, the *Tao Te Ching* cannot be earlier than Confucius' *Analects* (fifth century BC). The style of the *Tao Te Ching* is not that of question and answer, as are the *Analects* and the *Mencius*, so it is probably later than these works. Its style is that of the 'canon' (*ching*), a style not known prior to the Warring States Period (403–221 BC).[8] And Waley (1977, 125–8), writing in the 1930s, applied a linguistic analysis to the *Tao Te Ching* and similarly concluded that its grammar and vocabulary place it after the *Mencius*; that is, in the third century BC.

Any of these diverse facts, about the lack of reference to the *Tao Te Ching* in works of the period or a school of Lao Tzu, and about the style of the *Tao Te Ching*, taken in isolation would offer a most unsafe reason for dating the *Tao Te Ching* to the third century BC – but taken as a whole, they constitute a body of evidence which it would seem foolish to disregard. Until further facts come to light which add to or challenge our current knowledge it is fair and reasonable to conclude that Confucius and Lao Tzu never met, and granting that Lao Tzu really existed (and he may never have done so), he flourished no earlier than the third century BC:[9] at the very least, whoever actually compiled the *Tao Te Ching*, whether it was one man or several, the document almost certainly was not in circulation until the latter half of the third century BC.

Kaltenmark (1969, 13) observes that some passages in the *Tao Te Ching* are in rhyme whilst others are not. Those that rhyme do so in a variety of different meters. The anomalies that Kaltenmark finds when examining the rhymes can be accounted for only by supposing that the passages were written in different periods or in different regions. He concludes that the *Tao Te Ching* is an 'anthology of apothegms borrowed partly from the common stock of wisdom, partly from various proto-Taoist schools. The anthology was built up gradually and did not take on a more or less definitive form until the third century BC' (p. 14).

Fung Yu-lan (1983, 171) believes (in common with other scholars) that the founder of the philosophy expressed in the *Tao Te Ching* was probably Li Erh (third century BC), whom Ssu-ma Ch'ien when writing the *Shih Chi* confused with the legendary Lao Tan who was popularly identified with Lao Tzu, and this perpetuated the error that the *Tao Te Ching* originated three centuries earlier than it really did. The *Shih Chi* contains many biographical details about Li Erh, and it is reasonable to suppose that Li Erh was a real person and that many of these details are essentially accurate. It may be the case that Li Erh wrote the *Tao Te Ching*, or at least much of it, and it may be the case that he deliberately wrote under the name 'Lao Tzu' for two reasons. First, pretending that the legendary Lao Tzu was the author of the work would have lent it a prestige it may otherwise have lacked. This was a common practice in Europe during the Middle Ages and afterwards, when works on alchemy and other hermetic topics where frequently attributed to scholars who had lived in the ancient world, and sometimes to entirely mythical individuals, such as Hermes Trismegistos.[10] And second, the author of the *Tao Te Ching* in attributing his work to some long-dead scholar of a previous age would have been able to satisfy his Taoist inclination not to stand out and be noticed as a Sage.

So Lao Tzu and the precise origins of his school of Taoism remain elusive. We don't know whether the *Tao Te Ching* was created by one man or by several. Though, we have been able to conclude that the *Tao Te Ching* in the form that we now have it was written down and disseminated no earlier than the third century BC. This century falls at the second half of the Warring States Period, and a brief look at what was happening in China at this time will provide some insight into why the *Tao Te Ching* addresses the topics it does, and why it treats them in the way that it does. And to this extent we can see that the *Tao Te Ching* is very much a reaction to historical circumstances.[11]

Seventy-six years after the death of Confucius (551–479 BC), the state of Chin, which covered much of what is now northern China, split into warring factions. This inaugurated the Warring States Period which lasted 182 years, from 403 BC to 221 BC when the state of Ch'in (occupying much of present-day Kansu and Shensi)[12] succeeded in conquering the other states and established the first centralised imperial administration in China. Throughout this period, warfare was the common experience of everyone; at any one time up to seven large states were vying for overall supremacy. Whatever one's social status, life was uncertain and precarious. Whatever security you and your community might temporarily have enjoyed could be swept aside in an afternoon by the advance of an enemy army. New taxes could be levied, and your possessions requisitioned. If you had wealth, in a moment it was no longer yours. If you had sons who had been students or workers, in a moment they were conscripted and marched off.

Social and economic changes, which had started in the previous century, continued throughout the Warring States Period. One by one the feudal aristocracies lost their power, and the ordinary peasants were released from serfdom, gaining their independence. Anyone, even someone from a peasant background, could rise to a position of great political or military power. For the ambitious and the determined, opportunities for gaining wealth, power and fame abounded.[13]

In this historical milieu, intellectual development advanced as it had never done before. New philosophers, philosophies and schools appeared on the scene with unparalleled frequency. Indeed, there were so many schools that chroniclers of the period came to refer to them all simply as the 'Hundred Schools'. Scholars of the different schools travelled from state to state, offering their services to whomever were the rulers of the day.

Human institutions, especially governments who were responsible for funding and organising the continuous and seemingly endless inter-state wars, in the eyes of some of these scholars, became suspect and seen as the perverters of the natural order. Taoist thinkers in particular came to the view that ambition, especially political and military ambition, was the most dangerous and deadly of vices. If people would only live quietly, keeping to themselves, fitting in harmoniously with the natural order of things, then all the troubles that were month in month out constantly perplexing so many people would evaporate.

This is the essential message of the *Tao Te Ching*. Its advice and instructions are offered to all and sundry, but especially to rulers and those in positions of power, as the way by which one might survive and endure the turmoil and vicissitudes of the times, and make a proper example to others. *Action* was not required to put matters to rights: what was needed was the presence of mind to *refrain* from acting and doing things. If people had no ends to satisfy, they would not be pursuing the means to those ends which, in the Warring

States Period, were putting in jeopardy the well-being and lives of everyone.

It should be abundantly obvious to any intelligent person that the philosophy and advice of the *Tao Te Ching* is no less relevant to people living in today's troubled times than it was to Lao Tzu's contemporaries living in the third century BC.

STRUCTURE OF THE *TAO TE CHING*

Originally, the *Tao Te Ching* had no divisions. The current practice of dividing up the text into eighty-one chapters was first begun by editors and commentators in ancient times. In some instances, the divisions will be found to be arbitrary, grouping together sections of text that seem to deal with unconnected topics. Many chapters seem to be repeated, in part at least, elsewhere in the text, and it seems likely that sections of commentaries have become inadvertently incorporated into the text. Frequently terms such as 'therefore' and 'hence' introduce observations that cannot be logically derived from the preceding text. In short, the text is badly corrupted.

Despite this, from the text of the *Tao Te Ching* a startling, clear and essentially simple philosophy shines out. Precisely because this philosophy is simple, lacking the need for exposition in long and intellectually demanding discourse, the corruptions which earlier versions of the text have suffered make hardly any difference to the ease with which we can discern its insights.

TYPOGRAPHICAL PRESENTATION, AND INDEX

The division of the chapters of the *Tao Te Ching* into lettered sections is my own invention (inspired by Lao 1963), designed to make the locating of and reference to particular lines more easy. The value of this system will be apparent when the reader makes use of the Index to the *Tao Te Ching*.

I realised that this Index could be very useful. Whilst preparing the text for this book I frequently had lines of the *Tao Te Ching* come to mind, but couldn't remember where to find them. So I read through the *Tao Te Ching* from beginning to end, locating what I considered to be the key concepts and ideas, and listed against each the parts of the chapters where they occur. Thus, if for instance, we could vaguely recall the reference to spokes and hubs, we could look in the Index and find 'spokes *see* wheel' and 'wheel 11a'. Hopefully, including this Index will save the reader many frustrating minutes leafing through the entire *Tao Te Ching* trying to locate a particular, or half-remembered, reference.

NOTE TO THE READER

The point of this book is not just to present you with a new version of the *Tao Te Ching*, nor to move you towards a clearer understanding of what the ancient text says, but also to urge you to find a different outlook on yourself, your life and your aspirations. In urging you towards a fresh assessment of yourself and your needs, in helping you to identify what is of real importance and to leave behind what is trivial, this book aims to be a guide to living better, and to living well. But in living better for ourselves – at least in terms of what the *Tao Te Ching* teaches – you will also live better for everyone else and for the planet as a whole.

NOTES

1   or perhaps the San Pass, see Lau 1963, 123.
2   P. J. Lin (1977) calls the Keeper of the Pass 'Kuan Yin', whereas he is called 'Yin Hsi' by Maurer (1986) and by Waley (1977). The difficulty in deciding the Keeper's name arises because 'hsi' means 'delight', but this may be part of the Keeper's proper name. (If it is not, the text can be interpreted as recording that the Keeper greeted Lao Tzu with delight.) In written classical Chinese proper names are not indicated (as they are in English by capitalisation), and there is no punctuation to aid interpretation (see P. J. Lin 1977, 149).
3   The *Chuang Tzu* (named after its supposed author) stands with the *Tao Te Ching* as one of the most important sources of Taoist philosophy. In style it is very different from the *Tao Te Ching*, being written (mostly) in continuous prose, its many

different sections addressing distinct points or narrating fables which serve to illustrate specific ideas, some of which anticipate the style of later Zen writings.

4   Cf. 'Chuang Tzu', 'Mo Tzu', 'Lieh Tzu', and many others.

5   See Lau 1963, 97.

6   See Lau 1963, 97–8.

7   Apart from its mentioning the meeting between Confucius and Lao Tzu, Lao Tzu's name crops up several times in the *Chuang Tzu*, though only three times in the first seven chapters (these are the chapters which scholars confidently attribute to Chuang Tzu and which were written in the fourth century BC, contemporaneously with the *Mencius*; the other chapters are thought to be later additions). Yet nowhere does Lao Tzu appear to represent a school of thought or espouse any doctrines that we can recognise as quotations from or references to the *Tao Te Ching*. 'Lao Tzu' is just a name for an anonymous philosopher, along with scores of other names in the *Chuang Tzu*, which Chuang Tzu uses as his mouthpiece. Introducing all these different characters with their different names is just a literary device by means of which the author can set various points of view against each other. This literary technique is essentially the same as that adopted by Plato who wrote in ancient Greece in the fourth century BC.

8   See Fung Yu-lan 1983, 170.

9   Classical Chinese works should be regarded as anthologies of sayings added to by different thinkers at different times. The *Tao Te Ching* is not 'by' Lao Tzu in our modern sense of authorship at all. 'Lao Tzu' is best understood as 'from the school of Lao Tzu'. Later scholars and editors were quite happy to add extra material and to elaborate commentaries as they saw fit. This explains the *Tao Te Ching's* tendency to be repetitive (see Lau 1963, 106).

10   See Waley (1977, 102), who remarks that people at this time regarded books as repositories of important tradition whose function was to save such vital knowledge from being lost and forgotten. 'Consequently it was perfectly natural that when real authorship began writers should give their books the appearance of being records of ancient things, rather than present their ideas as new and personal discoveries.'

11   As indeed are many doctrines and philosophies.

12   Fung Yu-lan 1983, xviii.

13   See Fung Yu-lan 1983, 9–10.

Lao Tzu

Tao Te Ching

海鶴

1

a   The Tao that can be put in words is not the
                ever-abiding Tao;
       The name that can be named is not the ever-
                abiding name.
       The Nameless gives rise to Heaven and Earth.
       The Named is the Mother of the Ten
                Thousand Things.[1]

b   Therefore:
       It is always so that without desires you can
                behold its mystery;
       Always so that having desires you can behold
                its manifestations.
       These two[2] are one and the same, and differ
                only in name.
       This being so is profound, mysterious, and
                dark:
       The threshold to all secrets.

1   i.e. all things in existence.
2   i.e. the Nameless and the Named.

2

a   When all beneath Heaven[1] know beauty as
             beauty
There is ugliness.
When all know good as good
There is evil.

b   Thus being and non-being arise together;
Easy and difficult rely upon each other;
Long and short are dependent upon each
             other;
High and low contrast with each other;
Music and voice harmonise together.
Before and after follow each other.

c   Therefore the Sage acts by doing nothing and
             teaches without speaking.
The Ten Thousand Things arise, but he
             doesn't cause them to come.
They come into being, yet he claims no
             possession over them.
He works for their benefit, yet requires no
             gratitude.
He accomplishes his tasks, yet claims no merit.

d   Because he claims no merit, his merit does not
             leave him.

---

1 'Beneath Heaven' refers to the phenomenal world of everyday
experience.

3

a   Do not exalt the gifted, and the people will
              not be jealous.
        Do not prize rare treasures, and the people
              will not steal them.
        Do not display desirable things, and the
              hearts of the people will not be
              distracted.

b   Therefore the wise ruler:
        Empties their hearts and fills their bellies;
        Weakens their ambitions and strengthens
              their bones.
        He keeps the people without knowledge and
              free from desire
        So that those who know dare not act.
        He acts without acting and everything is kept
              in order.

4

a   The Tao is like an empty vessel, yet may be
              drawn from without ever needing to
              be filled.
        In its unfathomable depths arise the Ten
              Thousand Things.

b   It blunts sharp edges,
       Unties all tangles;
       It softens the glare
       And blends with the dust.[1]
       Hidden in the depths, perhaps it just seems to
              exist.
       Its origin is a mystery to me.
       It seems to be older than Heaven.

1   Waley (1977, 146) observes, 'Dust is the Taoist symbol for the
    noise and fuss of everyday life.' The Tao exists everywhere –
    even in *ch'en*, dust.

5

a   Heaven and Earth are not benevolent;
       They regard the Ten Thousand Things as
              straw dogs.[1]
       The Sage is not benevolent;
       He regards the Hundred Families[2] as straw
              dogs.

b   The space between Heaven and Earth is like a
              bellows:
       It is empty, yet not exhausted;
       The more it is used, the more it produces.

c   Many words exhaust themselves.
       It is better to watch over what is within.[3]

1   Straw dogs were made to be sacrificial offerings at religious
    ceremonies. Afterwards, having served their purpose, they would
    be thrown away and trampled under foot in the street or burned
    as fuel (see Ch'en Ku-ying 1977, 70; P. J. Lin 1977, 12; Wilhelm
    1985, 65; Welch 1966, 42; and Wieger 1988, 88).
2   i.e. all people.
3   presumably, the Tao. But the 'empty centre' may well be alluding
    to the bellows simile already introduced; if this is so, the 'empty
    centre' of the bellows should be likened to the space between
    Heaven and Earth. This space is where mankind dwells, and this
    line may be an exhortation discouraging people from presuming
    too much, or taking on tasks beyond their capacity. This interpre-
    tation at least accords with the general philosophy of the *Tao Te
    Ching*. See Welch (1966, 44–5) for an illuminating analysis of
    this chapter.

6

a   The Spirit of the Valley never dies.

        It is called the Mysterious Female.[1]

        The gate of the Mysterious Female is the

                source of Heaven and Earth.

        Ever-abiding, always existing,

        It can be used, but never exhausted.

1   presumably, the Mother of the Ten Thousand Things (which is
    the Tao itself). This chapter is obscure. Lau (1963, xxxviii–ix)
    suggests it echoes a primitive creation myth.

7

a   Heaven is eternal and Earth everlasting.

        They are eternal and everlasting because they

                do not exist for themselves,

        And thus they last forever.

b   This is why the Sage puts himself last, yet
             stays out ahead;
     He forgets himself and is thus preserved.
     Is this not because being selfless, he will
             thereby be fulfilled?

8

a   The superior man is like water.
     Water benefits the Ten Thousand Things,
             but does not compete with them.
     It stays in the places which people despise,
     And thus is close to Tao.

b   For his dwelling he chooses good ground;
             he has a mind that loves the profound;
             is benevolent when dealing with others;
             is sincere when he speaks;
             preserves order when ruling;
             shows competence in business;
             and takes action at the proper time.

c   Because he does not compete, he is beyond
             reproach.

9

a   Rather than fill the cup to the brim, it is better
        to stop in time.

b   The finely honed blade will soon lose its
        sharpness.
     Fill the hall with gold and jade, and no one
        can guard it.

c   Those who take pride in their wealth and
        honours, attract their own downfall.
     To stop when the task is finished is the Way
        of Heaven.

10

a   Can you embrace the oneness of everything
        with body and soul
     Without being distracted?
     When concentrating your breath to bring
        about softness,
     Can you be like a baby?
     Can you clean your profound mirror and
        make it free from blemish?[1]
     Can you love the people and rule the country
     Yet be without knowledge?
     When the gates of Heaven open and close[2]
     Can you keep to the role of the female?[3]

When your intelligence has penetrated to the
              four corners
Can you refrain from acting?

b   To produce things and nourish them;
       To bring them forth without possessing them;
       To benefit them without reward,
       And lead without imposing,
       Is called profound Virtue.

1   this may allude to a meditation technique. The 'profound mirror'
    is a simile for the mind; making it 'free from blemish' is to avoid
    making emotional responses to the events and circumstances of
    the everyday world.
2   perhaps, simply, 'when things happen'.
3   i.e. remain passive and refrain from acting.

11

a   Thirty spokes are fixed to the hub;
       It is the hole in the hub which makes the
              wheel useful.

b   Clay can be shaped into a vessel;
       But it is the space inside which gives it its
              usefulness.

c   Doors and windows are cut out to make a
              room;
       The room is useful only because of the holes.

d   Therefore, gain from what does exist,

         And make use of what doesn't exist.

12

a   The five colours blind the eyes;[1]

         The five notes deafen the ears;[2]

         The five tastes spoil the palate;[3]

         Riding and hunting madden the mind;

         Rare treasure will distract one from the path.

b   Therefore the Sage provides for his inner

             needs, and not for his eyes.

         Thus he rejects one and chooses the other.

1   The five primary colours are: red, yellow, green or blue, black and white.

2   The five notes of the Chinese pentatonic scale are: C, D, E, G and A.

3. The five tastes are: sweet, sour, bitter, acrid, and salty.

13

a   Favour and disgrace equally cause
           apprehension.
       Fortune and misfortune have their origin in
           our own bodies.

b   What is meant by saying that favour and
           disgrace equally cause apprehension?
       Favour is for inferior people:
       Being favoured leads to the apprehension of
           losing favour,
       And losing it leads to the fear of greater
           misfortune.
       This means that favour and disgrace equally
           cause apprehension.

c   What is meant by saying that fortune and
           misfortune have their origin in our
           own bodies?
       Having a body, I am liable to misfortune;
       If I had no body, what misfortune could I
           suffer?

d   Therefore, he who values the world as much
           as his own body
       Is fit to rule the empire.
       And he who loves the world as much as his
           own body

May be entrusted to care for all beneath
    Heaven.

14

a   Looked for, it cannot be seen:
         it is not visible.
      Listened for, it cannot be heard:
         it makes no sound.
      Grasped at, it cannot be held:
         it is not tangible.
      These three[1] are beyond scrutiny.
      But they are blended in the One.

b   On top it is not bright;
      Underneath it is not dark.
      It is unceasing and cannot be named;
      It returns to nothingness.
      It is called the formless form
      And the imageless image.
      That is why it is called obscure and indistinct.

c   Go to meet it, and you will find no
         beginning.
      Follow after it, and you will find no end.
      Hold to the ancient Tao
      In order to manage events in the present.

d   Knowing the ancient beginning
         Is called holding to Tao's thread.[2]

1   i.e. the three qualities of being invisible, soundless, and intan-
    gible.
2   or following the principle/system/tradition of Tao.

15

a   In ancient times masters of the Tao were
                  possessed of a subtle mystery and a
                  penetrating perception;
         Too profound to be understood.
         Because they were too profound to be
                  understood,
         All we can do is describe their outward
                  appearance:
                  Cautious, like one crossing a river in
                           winter;
                  Hesitant, like one who fears his
                           neighbours;
                  Reserved, like one who is a guest;
                  Yielding, like ice that is melting;
                  Simple, like an uncarved block;
                  Open, like a wide valley;
                  Obscure, like muddy water.

b   Who can make muddy water clear by
                  keeping still?
         Who can, from rest, gradually stir to life?[1]

Those who hold fast to the Tao

Have no desire to be filled.

Having no desire to be filled

They can endure all wear yet never need to be
    renewed.

1   These two lines may allude to a meditation technique (LaFarge
1994, 357).

16

a   Become completely empty.

Hold firm to stillness.

The Ten Thousand Things come to life, then
    return whence they came:

They increase and flourish, but each returns
    to its source.

Returning to the source is stillness; it is what
    is destined.

What is destined is unchanging.

To know what is unchanging is to have
    insight;

Being ignorant of what is unchanging leads to
    misfortune.

b   He who knows what is unchanging will be
    impartial.

He who is impartial will act justly.

He who acts justly is like a good ruler.

He who is a good ruler is in accord with
Heaven.
He who is in accord with Heaven is in accord
with the Tao.
He who is in accord with the Tao is
everlasting;
And to the end of his days, he will meet with
no danger.

17

a   The best rulers are those whom the people
hardly know exist.
Next come rulers whom the people love and
praise.
After that come rulers whom the people fear.
And the worst rulers are those whom the
people despise.

b   The ruler who does not trust the people will
not be trusted by the people.

c   The best ruler stays in the background, and
his voice is rarely heard.
When he accomplishes his tasks, and things
go well,
The people declare: It was we who did it by
ourselves.

18

a   When Tao is abandoned,

Benevolence and morality arise.

When wisdom and knowledge arise,

Hypocrisy flourishes.

b   When there is discord in the family,[1]

Filial piety and parental affection arise.

When the country is in darkness and turmoil,

Loyal ministers appear.

1   *Strictly*, 'when the six family relationships are not in harmony'. These are the relationships of father and son, elder brother and younger brother, and husband and wife. (This conception of family relationships is clearly gender-biased, leaving out of account mothers, daughters and sisters.)

七筆破雙个字

19

a   Give up sagacity and abandon knowledge,
And the people will benefit a hundredfold.
Give up benevolence and abandon morality,
And the people will return to natural
      affection.
Give up scheming and abandon gain,
And robbers and thieves will disappear.

b   These words in themselves are inadequate.
Therefore let the following be appended:
     Exhibit plainness,
     Embrace the simple,
     Reduce self-interest,
     Curb desire.

20

a   Abandon learning and put an end to sorrow.[1]
What is the difference between 'yes' and
      'no'?
What is the difference between good and evil?
Should I fear what others fear
There would be no end to my fear.
The people are happy, as if enjoying the
      sacrificial feast,

Or at springtime climbing the terrace in the
    park.
But I alone am unmoved, showing no
    sentiment,
Like a baby who has yet to learn how to
    smile.
I am alone and have no home to go to.

b   Others have more than they need,
Whilst I have nothing.
Mine is the mind of a fool,
Completely muddled!
Others see things so clear cut,
Whilst I am confused.
They see so many differences,
Whilst I see no distinctions.
I am as one adrift on the sea;
I am like a restless wind with no direction.

c   The people all have a purpose,
Whilst I am aimless and depressed.
I alone am different from the others;
I value seeking nourishment from the
    Mother.[2]

1   This line probably belongs at the end of the previous chapter.
2   i.e. the Tao.

21

a   In all that he does, a man of great Virtue
         follows Tao and Tao alone.
Tao is invisible and intangible.
It is invisible and intangible, yet within is
         form.
It is intangible and invisible, yet within is
         substance.
It is dim and obscure, yet within is essence.
This essence is perfectly genuine, and from it
         faith emerges.

b   From ancient times until now, its name has
         not been forgotten,
Since it is perceived in the source of all
         things.
How do I know that this is the true nature of
         things?
Through Tao.

22

a   That which yields will be preserved.
That which bends will be straight.
That which is empty will be filled.
That which wears out will be renewed.

He who has little will gain more.
He who has much will be perplexed.

b   Therefore the Sage embraces the oneness of
        the Tao,
And sets an example to everyone.
He does not make a great show, therefore he
        shines out.
He does not try to justify himself, and so he
        is distinguished.
He does not boast, so receives merit.
He is not arrogant, and so endures.
Because he does not compete, no one under
        Heaven can compete with him.

c   When the ancients said, 'Yield and be
        preserved,' was that an empty
        saying?
Attain completeness, and all things will come
        to you.

23

a   To speak little is natural.
A high wind will not last all morning,
And a sudden downpour will not last all day.
And why is this?
Heaven and Earth have made it so.

If Heaven and Earth cannot make things
      which last forever,
How much less is it possible for man?

b   Therefore those who follow the Tao will be
         at one with the Tao.
Those who exercise Virtue will be at one with
      Virtue.
Those who lose them will be at one with their
      loss.

c   At one with the Tao, Tao welcomes you.
At one with Virtue, Virtue welcomes you.
At one with your loss, loss welcomes you.

d   Those who do not trust others
Will not themselves be trusted.

24

a   Those who stand on tiptoe are not steady.
Those who stride out ahead will soon fall
      behind.

b   Those who make a big show are far from
      enlightenment.
Those who think they can never be wrong are
      not respected.

Those who justify themselves have no merit.
Those who boast will not last long.

c   To followers of the Tao, such actions are
         excessive, like eating too much.
They are disliked by all things,
And therefore followers of the Tao do not seek
         refuge in them.

25

a   There is something formless yet complete
Which existed before Heaven and Earth.
Silent and fathomless,
Alone and unchanging;
Inexhaustible and pervading everywhere,
It may be thought of as the Mother of all
         under Heaven.
I do not know its name; I shall call it Tao.
If pressed for a description, I would call it
         Great.

b   Being great is to go ever-onward.
Going ever-onward is to reach everywhere.
Reaching everywhere is to return.

c   Therefore Tao is great;
Heaven is great;

Earth is great;
The King is also great.
The universe contains four great things,
And one of them is the King.
Man follows Earth;
Earth follows Heaven;
Heaven follows Tao;
And Tao follows what is naturally so.

26

a   Seriousness is the basis of levity.
Stillness is the master of restlessness.

b   Therefore the sage, travelling all day,
Does not lose sight of his baggage-wagon.
Though there are magnificent sights to be
      seen, he remains calm and detached.

c   Why would it be that the ruler of ten
      thousand chariots would act lightly in
      public?
To be light-hearted is to lose one's
      foundation.
To be restless is to lose control.

27

a   A good traveller leaves no tracks.
     A good speaker cannot be refuted.
     A good reckoner needs no abacus.
     A good door needs neither lock nor bolt;
     Yet it cannot be opened.
     A good binding needs neither rope nor
              knots;
     Yet it cannot be untied.

b   Therefore the Sage excels in taking care of
              everyone,
     And no one is forgotten.
     He excels in finding a use for everything,
     Hence nothing is rejected.
     This is called practising enlightenment.

c   Therefore the good man is the teacher of the
              bad;
     And the bad man is the material upon which
              the good man works.
     He who does not value the teacher
     And cherish the subject-matter,
     Regardless of his learning, has gone astray.
     This is called the ultimate mystery.

28

a   He who knows the masculine and keeps to
            the feminine
     Will be the river of the world.[1]
     Being the river of the world
     He will never be separated from eternal
            Virtue,[2]
     Becoming once again a little child.

b   He who knows the white and keeps to the
            black
     Will be an example for the whole world.
     Being an example for the whole world
     He will never stray from eternal Virtue,
     And he will return to the infinite.

c   He who knows honour and keeps to the
            humble
     Will be the valley of the world.
     Being the valley of the world
     He will be content with eternal Virtue,
     And become like an uncarved block.[3]

d   When the block is carved, it is made into
            useful things.
     And when the Sage makes use of them, he
            becomes the ruler.

It is the best carver who does the least

cutting.

1   i.e. as all moisture flows to the main river, so all the people will come to the Sage to be enlightened.
2   i.e. he will be in accord with the Tao, in accord with the way things are naturally meant to be.
3   i.e. the most simple of things, uninfluenced by conscious actions.

29

a   Would it be possible to take charge of the
                world and make it better than it is?
    I do not believe that such a thing is possible.

b   Since the world is sacred
    No improvements can be made.
    If you try to change it, you will spoil it.
    If you try to grasp it, you will lose it.

c   So, there are times
          for forging ahead, and for staying behind;
          for keeping silent, and for speaking aloud.
    Some are strong, while others are weak;
    Some rejoice, while others lament.

d   This is why the Sage avoids excess, extremes,
          and extravagance.

30

a   He who advises the ruler in the Way of Tao
   Advises against the use of military force to
      conquer the world.
   Adopting force will invite resistance.
   Where armies camp, brambles and thorns
      grow.
   Years of bad harvests come after a great war.

b   A good ruler does what is needed, then stops,
   Never daring to conquer the world.
   So do what is needed without bragging.
   Do what is needed without boasting.
   Do what is needed without being arrogant.
   Do what is needed, but only when there is
      no other way.
   Do what is needed without using violence.
   Use of violence is followed by defeat.

c   Such action is contrary to Tao,
   And what is contrary to Tao soon comes to
      an early end.

31

a   Fine weapons are the instruments of evil,
              hateful to all.
      So those with Tao spurn them.
      Men of peace favour the left;
      Men of war favour the right.

b   Weapons are the tools of misfortune;
      They are not the choice of the wise man,
      Who uses them only when there is no other
              way;
      And even then, he acts with calm restraint,
      And victory is no occasion for rejoicing.

c   To rejoice in victory is to delight in killing.
      Those who enjoy slaughter cannot find
              fulfilment in the world.

d   Auspicious occasions honour the left-hand
                place;
        Inauspicious occasions honour the right-hand
                place.[1]
        The second-in-command stands on the left,
        Whilst the commander-in-chief stands on the
                right,
        Arranged as they would be at rites of
                mourning.
        When so many have been slaughtered,
        Let us mourn with tears of sorrow,
        And treat victory like a funeral.

1   The left-hand side is considered the honourable side, and the
    right-hand side is considered the less honourable (see Maurer
    1986, 93).

32

a   Tao is eternally nameless.
        Although, as an uncarved block,[1] it is small,
        None under Heaven can subjugate it.
        If kings and lords could take possession of it,
        Of their own accord the Ten Thousand
                Things would pay them homage.
        Heaven and Earth would come together,
        And sweet rain fall.
        Peace and order would spread among the
                people
        Without its being decreed.

b   When the block is cut, the parts need names.
Are there not already enough names?
One should know when to stop.
Knowing when to stop, one avoids all
      danger.

c   Tao in the world is like a river flowing to the
      sea.

1   i.e. as a very simple, undifferentiated thing.

33

a   He who knows others is wise;
He who knows himself is enlightened.
Conquering others requires force;
Conquering oneself requires strength.

b   He who is content is rich.
To act with perseverance requires will-power.
He who stays where he is, endures.
To die but not be forgotten is to enjoy long
      life.

34

a   The great Tao flows everywhere,
     Going to the left and to the right.
     The Ten Thousand Things depend upon it
             for life;
     It denies itself to none of them,
     Accomplishing its task
     But claiming no credit.

b   It clothes and feeds the Ten Thousand
             Things,
     Yet does not claim to be their master.
     Forever without desire, it may be called
             small.

c   The Ten Thousand Things return to it,
     Yet it does not claim possession over them:
     Thus it may be called great.

d   Because it never strives for greatness,
     It thereby accomplishes greatness.

35

a   To he who holds the great image,
     The whole world will come.

They will come and meet with no harm,
Finding safety, tranquillity and comfort.

b   Music and food will induce the passer-by to
        stop,
     But when the Tao is spoken of in words, it
        seems bland and tasteless.
     Looked for, it cannot be seen.
     Listened for, it cannot be heard.
     Use it, and it can never be exhausted.

36

a   Whatever shrinks
Must first have expanded.
Whatever becomes weak
Must first have been strong.
That which will be destroyed
Must first have flourished.
In order to receive,
One must first give.

b   This is called seeing the nature of things.
The soft overcomes the hard, and the weak
overcomes the strong.

c   As fish cannot be taken from the water,
So a ruler should not reveal to the people his
means of government.

37

a   The Tao never acts,
Yet nothing is left undone.
If the ruler were able to hold to it,
The Ten Thousand Things would take shape
of their own accord.

b   If in taking shape, desire should arise,
      He would quell it by means of the nameless
            simplicity.
      With the nameless simplicity
      There will be no desires.
      Being free from desire, tranquillity is
            attained,
      And everything beneath Heaven will be at
            peace.

38

a   The truly good man is unaware of his
               goodness,
      And thus is good.
      The foolish man sets himself to be good,
      And so is not good.

b   The truly good man takes no action,
      Yet all things are accomplished.
      The foolish man is forever taking action,
      And much is left undone.

c   The truly benevolent man acts without
               striving to satisfy personal ends;
      Yet the seeker of morality acts with an
               ulterior motive.
      And when the follower of rules takes action
               and no one responds,
      He rolls up his shirt-sleeves to impose order
               by force.

d   Therefore, when Tao is lost, goodness
               remains.
      When goodness is lost, benevolence remains.
      When benevolence is lost, morality remains.
      When morality is lost, rules remain.
      Merely following rules[1] is a pretence of trust

and loyalty, and is the beginning of
confusion.

To seek knowledge of the future is to hold to
a false Tao, and is the beginning of
folly.

e   Therefore the superior man holds to the real
And ignores mere appearances;
Takes the fruit and rejects the flower;
Accepts the first and discards the second.

1   i.e. adhering to Confucian Rites.

39

a   These are the things of ancient times which
obtained the One:[1]
Heaven obtained the One and became clear;
Earth obtained the One and became stable;
The Gods obtained the One and became
divine;
The Valleys obtained the One and became
full;
The Ten Thousand Things obtained the One
and were made alive;
Kings and lords obtained the One and ruled
the empire.
Did they not all become as they are by
obtaining the One?

b   Without clarity,
          Heaven would soon shatter.
      Without stability,
          the Earth would soon split.
      Without being divine,
          the Gods would soon dissolve.
      Without being full,
          the Valleys would soon be exhausted.
      Without life,
          the Ten Thousand Things would soon
              perish.
      Without kings and lords,
          the empire would soon fall.

c   Therefore the noble has its root in the
              humble.
      The high has its foundation in the low.
      This is why kings and lords call themselves
              orphaned, lonely, and without
              sustenance.
      Thus they regard the humble as their root.

d   Those who are most praiseworthy
      Do not need praise.
      They prefer neither to be rare, like jade,
      Nor common, like stone.

1   i.e. the Tao.

40

a   The motion of Tao is to return.
    The Way of Tao is to yield.

b   The Ten Thousand Things have their source
              in being;
    Being arises from non-being.

41

a   When the superior man hears of the Tao, he
              practises it diligently.
    When the average man hears about the Tao,
              he follows it only intermittently.
    When the foolish man hears of the Tao, he
              bursts out laughing.
    But for this laughter Tao would not be Tao.

b   Hence, the ancients have said:
    The lightest path seems to be dark;
    Going forward seems like going back;
    The easy way seems to be hard;
    The highest Virtue seems empty;
    That which is pure seems sullied;
    Ample Virtue appears inadequate;

Strength to be had from Virtue seems
      lacking;
Virtue itself appears unreal.

c   The greatest space has no corners;
The greatest talent develops slowly;
The loudest sound cannot be heard;
The greatest form has no shape.

d   Tao is hidden and without a name;
Yet it is Tao which nourishes all things and
      brings everything to completion.

42

a   Tao gives birth to one;
One gives birth to two;
Two gives birth to three;[1]
And three gives birth to the Ten Thousand
      Things.

b   The Ten Thousand Things carry yin and
      embrace yang;
And by blending these vital forces, they
      achieve harmony.

c   The people hate being orphaned, lonely, and
      without sustenance,

Even though this is how kings and lords
describe themselves.

d   One may gain by losing
And lose by gaining.

e   I teach what others have taught:
'Those who are violent do not die a natural
death.'
I shall make this the basis of my teaching.

1   Perhaps 'two' is 'non-being', and 'three', 'being', or 'two', 'yin',
and 'three', 'yang'. But see also Wilhelm (1985, 21 and 73) who
suggests that 'one' is the unity in which all opposites are 'inter-
mingled', and which generates 'two' 'as antithesis (the opposites
of light and dark, male and female ...). From these pairs of
opposites the phenomenal world is born as the Three' (p. 21).
However we understand the numbers, this part of the chapter
points to the multiplicity of things having their source in the undifferentiated Tao.

43

a   Under Heaven, it is the softest things which
overcome the hardest things.
That which has no substance can penetrate
where there is no room.
Thus I know the benefit of non-action.

b   Few in the world understand the advantage of
Teaching without words and accomplishing
without action.

44

a   Fame or self: which is the most dear?
Self or wealth: which has most value?
Gain or loss: which is worse?

b   Attachment to things results in wasteful
            expense.
The more that is hoarded, the heavier the
            loss.
Know contentment and thus never be
            disappointed;
Know when to stop and thus avoid all
            danger.
This is the way to last forever.

45

a   Great accomplishment seems inadequate,
But its usefulness will last forever.
Great fullness seems empty,
But using it cannot exhaust it.

b   Great straightness seems crooked.
Great skill seems awkward.
Great surplus seems deficient.
Great eloquence seems to stammer.

c Movement overcomes cold.
  Stillness overcomes heat.
  Being calm and tranquil one can become ruler
    of the world.

46

a When Tao is present in the world
  Racehorses are taken off to work in the
    fields.
  When Tao is absent from the world
  War-horses are bred in the countryside.

b There is no crime greater than having desires.
  No disaster is greater than not being content
    with one's lot.
  The worst misfortune is to be greedy.
  He who is content with what he has
  Has enough.

47

a Without going out of doors
  One can know the whole world.
  Without looking through the window
  One can see the Way of Heaven.
  The further one goes,
  The less one knows.

b   Thus the Sage knows without going out;
Understands without looking;
And accomplishes without acting.

48

a   In pursuit of knowledge, something new is
learned every day.
In pursuit of the Tao, something is
abandoned every day.

b   Do less and less
Until non-action is achieved.
Do nothing, and nothing remains undone.

c   All things can be accomplished by not acting.
The empire can never be governed by taking
action.

49

a   The Sage has no mind of his own;
He makes the mind of the people his mind.

b   Treat well those who are good;
Treat well those who are not good.
Thus everyone will become good.
Trust those who are sincere;
Trust those who are not sincere.
Thus everyone will become sincere.

c   When dealing with the world, the Sage
blends his mind harmoniously
with the mind of the people.
The people all watch him and listen to his
words.
He accepts them all as his children.

50

a   Between being born and dying
Three out of ten are companions of life;
Three out of ten are companions of death.
And three out of ten in their lives progress
from activity to death;
Why is this?
Because they strive too intensely after life.[1]

b   It is well known that those who know how
                to live properly can go out
      Without fear of meeting rhinoceros or tiger.
      Caught in the fray, weapons cannot harm
                them.
      The rhinoceros cannot gore them with its
                horn;
      The tiger cannot maul them with its claws;
      And weapons can find no place to pierce.
      Why is this?
      For them there is no such thing as death.

1   All translators find these lines particularly hard to interpret.
    'Three out of ten' presumably means 'one third' (see Lau 1963,
    57). Henricks notes (1990, 122) that these lines can be taken to
    mean 'roughly speaking, one-third of humanity seems to be born
    to ... live a long time no matter what they do; another third
    seems born fated to ... die young no matter what they do; and,
    finally, another third can live long or die young depending on how
    they live, but they hasten their journey to death with their anxiety
    to hold on to life'. (Henricks, reluctantly, favours a different inter-
    pretation, based on his own, different, preferred translation of
    this chapter. His reasons for preferring his different translation
    are quite involved and technical, and cannot be gone into here
    (see Henricks 1990, 123).

      51

a   Tao gives rise to all things;
      Virtue nourishes them;
      Environment shapes them;
      Circumstances complete them.
      Therefore the Ten Thousand Things

Respect Tao and honour Virtue.
No one commands that
Tao be respected and Virtue honoured.
Doing so comes spontaneously.

b   So it is that all things arise from Tao;
They are nourished by Virtue,
Grown and nurtured,
Given shelter and comfort,
Matured and protected.
Tao produces them but does not possess
        them;
Accomplishes without taking credit;
Guides without interfering.
This is called mystical Virtue.

52

a   All things under Heaven have the same
        source;
This may be called the Mother of the Ten
        Thousand Things.
Knowing the mother,
One may know the children.
Knowing the children,
One may keep to the mother,
And to the end of one's days, never meet
        with danger.

b   Whosoever closes the mouth
And shuts the doors[1]
Will be free from trouble throughout his life.
But whosoever opens the mouth
And adds to his affairs,
To the end of his days, will be beyond hope.

c   To see the small is to be enlightened.
To keep to the weak is to be strong.
Use the light of your intellect,
But return to enlightenment,
And thus avoid misfortune.
This is called practising the constant.

1   of the senses.

53

a   Having just a little intelligence
I would keep to the main road,[1]
My only fear that I might stray from it.
It is easy to keep to the main road,
But the people prefer the by-ways.

b   When the court is maintained in lavish
          splendour,
The fields are full of weeds
And the granaries are empty.
Some wear extravagant clothes

And carry sharp swords.

They consume food and drink to excess

And accumulate more wealth and possessions
      than they can find use for.

This is called robbery and extravagance,

And is contrary to Tao.

1   i.e. follow Tao.

54

a   What is well-planted cannot be uprooted;

     What is grasped tightly cannot slip away;

     Just as ancestral sacrifices will never be
          suspended.

b   Cultivate Tao in yourself
          and Virtue will be real.

     Cultivate it in the family
          and Virtue will be plentiful.

     Cultivate it in the community
          and Virtue will increase.

     Cultivate it in the state
          and Virtue will flourish.

     Cultivate it in the world
          and Virtue will be universal.

c   Hence, judge a person as a person,

     A family as a family,

A community as a community,
A state as a state,
The world as a world.

d   How do I know the world is like this?
        Through observation.

55

a   He who possesses Virtue in abundance is like
                a newly born infant.
        Poisonous insects will not sting him;
        Wild beasts will not seize him;
        Birds of prey will not attack him.
        His bones are soft, his muscles weak, but his
                grasp is strong.
        He has not experienced the union of male
                and female,
        And yet is fully virile:
        His essence is complete.
        He can cry all day without getting hoarse.
        This is harmony at its height.

b   Knowing harmony is to know what is
                eternal.
        Knowing what is eternal is to be enlightened.

c   It is inauspicious to try to improve on life,
And harmful to regulate breathing by
      conscious control.
To strive for too much results in exhaustion.
These actions are contrary to Tao.
And what is contrary to Tao soon comes to
      an early end.

56

a   He who knows does not speak.
He who speaks does not know.
He closes the mouth
And shuts the doors;[1]
Blunts sharp edges,
Unties all tangles;
Softens the glare,
And blends with the dust.
This is called mystical union.

b   He who can attain this state[2]
Is not concerned with being liked or
      disliked,
Benefited or harmed,
Exalted or despised.
Thus he is valued by the world.

1   of the senses.
2   of being like a Sage.

57

a   Rule the state with integrity.
Wage war[1] with cunning strategy;
But win the empire through non-action.
How do I know this?
By this:

b   The more rules and regulations there are,
    the more poor the people become.
The more sharp weapons there are,
    the more troubled the state becomes.
The more clever the people become,
    the more cunning will their actions
        become.
The more that law and order is promoted,
    the more thieves and robbers there will
        be.

c   Therefore the Sage says:
    I do not act and the people transform
        themselves.
    I love tranquillity and the people rectify
        themselves.
    I do nothing and the people prosper by
        themselves.
    I have no desires and the people become
        like an uncarved block, returning to
        simplicity by themselves.

1   presumably, 'Only when there is no other way' (31b).

58

a   When the government is unobtrusive,
The people are content and honest.
When the government is severe and exacting,
The people are restless and cunning.

b   Good fortune has its roots in misfortune,
And misfortune lurks beneath good fortune.
Who knows the limits of this?
Is anything as it appears to be?
What is normal becomes abnormal,
And what is auspicious becomes ominous.
This being so has perplexed people for a long
    time.

c   Therefore the Sage is pointed like a square,
    but does not pierce.
He is sharp like a knife, but does not cut.[1]
He is straight like a stick, but does not
    extend himself.
He is bright like light, but does not dazzle.

1   The Sage is intellectually penetrating, but he does not show up other people's muddledness.

59

a   When ruling the people and serving Heaven,
There is nothing better than restraint.
In being restrained, one may follow Tao
      from the beginning.
Following Tao from the beginning is to
      accumulate great Virtue.
Accumulating great Virtue there is nothing
      that cannot be overcome.
When there is nothing that cannot be
      overcome, there are no limits.
Knowing no limits, one can rule the state.
Possessing the Mother[1] of the state,
      one will long endure.

b   This is called having deep roots and a firm
      stalk,
And is the way to long life and lasting vision.

1   'Mother' here may mean 'Tao' (see Chan 1969, 164 n. 97).

60

a   Ruling a large country is like cooking a small
         fish.[1]

b   When the empire is ruled in accord with Tao,
      The evil spirits will lose their power.
      Not that the evil spirits will lose their powers
         entirely,
      But they will not do any harm to anyone.
      Not only do the evil spirits do no harm,
      Neither does the Sage.
      Since neither these two powers[2] do any harm
         to the people,
      Virtue is accumulated as they unite in their
         effect.[3]

1   i.e. the fish is spoilt if the cook disturbs it or is too hasty (see
    Wang Pi's commentary in P. J. Lin 1977, 122). Lau points out
    (1963, 76) that a small fish is spoilt simply by handling it.
2   i.e. the Sage, and the evil spirits.
3   See Wang Pi's commentary in P. J. Lin 1977, 112–13.

61

a   A large state is like low-lying land where the
         flowing waters meet:[1]
      The female of the world.

b   It is the stillness of the feminine which
                overcomes the masculine.
     Keeping still is to keep to the lower position.

c   Therefore the large state can conquer the
                small state by giving way to the small
                state.
     And the small state can conquer the large
                state by submitting to the large state.

d   Thus, in order to conquer one must yield,
     And those who conquer do so by yielding.
     Since the large state wishes to take in more
                people,
     And the small state wishes to serve the
                people,
     Both have their wishes met.
     It is right for a large state to yield.

1   i.e. the centre to which all things tend to gravitate.

62

a   The Ten Thousand Things have their source
                in the Tao.
     It is the treasure of the good man, and the
                refuge of the bad.
     Fine words can purchase honour.
     Good deeds can earn respect.

Even if a man is bad, that is no reason to
    abandon him.

b   Therefore when the Son of Heaven[1] is
        crowned and the three ministers
        installed,
    Rather than offering gifts of jade discs and a
        team of four horses,
    It is better to remain seated and offer the
        Tao.

c   Why did the ancients value the Tao so
        highly?
    Did they not say, 'By means of the Tao,
        Those who seek it shall find it, and the
        guilty shall be forgiven'?
    This is why it is so valued by the world.

1 i.e. the Emperor.

63

a   Act by not acting.
    Work without effort.
    Savour the tasteless.
    See much in the few and greatness in the
        small.
    Reward injury with kindness.

b   Plan the difficult while it is still easy.
     Accomplish greatness in small things.

c   Under Heaven, difficult things consist of easy
         things.
     Under Heaven, great actions consist of small
         deeds.
     The Sage never attempts anything great,
     And thus accomplishes greatness.

d   He who takes his promises lightly will not be
         trusted.
     He who thinks everything is easy will meet
         many difficulties.
     This is why the Sage regards everything as
         difficult,
     And therefore never meets with any
         difficulties.

   64

a   Things which keep still are easy to hold.
     Events yet to happen are easy to plan.
     Things that are fragile are easy to break.
     Things that are small are easy to lose.

b   Deal with things before they happen.
     Put things in order before chaos sets in.

c   A tree as big as a man's embrace grows from
        a tiny shoot;
     A nine-storey terrace begins as a mound of
        earth;
     A journey of a thousand miles starts with the
        first step.

d   Those who take action, fail.
     Those who grasp for things, lose them.
     Therefore the Sage takes no action, yet never
        fails;
     He grasps for nothing, yet never loses.

e   In managing their affairs people often fail at
        the point of success.
     So attend carefully to the end as much as to
        the beginning,
     And there will be no failure.

f   Therefore the Sage desires to be free from
        desire.
     He does not prize rare treasures.
     He learns to unlearn his learning,
     And he brings the people back to what they
        have lost.[1]
     Thus he furthers the natural completion of
        the Ten Thousand Things,
     And refrains from acting.

1   i.e., the Tao

65

a   In ancient times, those who excelled in the
    pursuit of Tao did not seek to
    enlighten people, but to keep them in
    their natural state of ignorance.
The reason for this is that when people have
    too much knowledge they are difficult
    to govern.

b   Therefore, those who rule by increasing
    knowledge, do so to the detriment of
    the state;
And those who rule by decreasing
    knowledge, do so to the benefit of the
    state.
Knowing these two things is to follow the
    ancient standard.
To follow the ancient standard is called
    mystical Virtue.
Mystical Virtue is deep and far reaching.
By its practise, all things return to their
    original natural state
Of complete harmony.

66

a   Rivers and seas become the kings of the
              hundred streams
      Because they keep to the lower position.
      Thus they become their kings.

b   Therefore the Sage, wishing to rule over the
              people,
      Must use humble words before them;
      And wishing to lead the people,
      He must keep himself behind them.

c   Thus the Sage rules over the people, and they
              do not feel oppressed;
      He leads the people, and they do not feel
              obstructed.

d   Therefore all beneath Heaven support him
              and do not tire of him.
      Because he does not compete, no one can
              compete with him.

67

a   All under Heaven say that my Tao is great
              and resembles nothing.[1]
      Because it is great, it resembles nothing.

If it did resemble anything, it would a long
time ago have become small.

b   There are three treasures which I keep and
value.
The first is compassion;
The second is frugality;
And the third is not daring to be ahead of
others.
Being compassionate, one can be courageous.
Being frugal, one can be generous.
Not daring to be ahead of others, one can
lead the world.

c   But nowadays, there are those who abandon
compassion, yet wish to be
courageous;
They reject frugality, yet wish to be
generous;
They forsake not daring to be ahead of
others, yet wish to lead the world.
Their downfall is certain.

d   Being compassionate, one will win in attack
and be strong in defence.
By giving compassion, Heaven provides and
protects.[2]

---

1   i.e. the Tao cannot be compared to or likened to any of the
things normally experienced.

2   This line is ambiguous between 'Heaven is compassionate in providing and protecting' and 'The way that Heaven provides and protects is by making men compassionate' (see Feng and English 1973, and Lau 1963, for the latter interpretation, and Chan 1969, and Ch'u 1985, for the former).

68

a   He who makes a good soldier is not violent.
He who makes a good fighter is not angry.
He who makes a good conqueror does not
     compete.[1]
He who is skilful in making the best use of
     people, places himself under them.

b   This is called the Virtue of not competing.
This is called making use of people.
This is called matching the sublimity of
     Heaven.[2]

1   i.e. he overcomes his enemies without the need to fight them.
2   i.e. accomplishing things, like Heaven, without striving.

69

a   The strategists have a saying:
>   'I dare not take the offensive, but would
>   rather take the defensive.[1]
>   'I dare not advance an inch, but would
>   rather retreat a foot.'

b   This is called marching without moving,
>   Rolling up one's sleeve without showing
>   one's arm,
>   Defeating an enemy without confrontation,
>   Being armed without weapons.

c   No misfortune is greater than
>   underestimating an enemy.
>   Underestimating my enemy almost makes me
>   lose my treasures.[2]

d   Therefore, when two sides takes arms against
>   each other,
>   It is the side with the most reluctance which
>   wins.

1 *Strictly*, 'I dare not be the host, but would rather be the guest.'
   That is, the host, being at home, must take the initiative, and is in
   this sense active whereas the guest takes the passive role.
2 Wang Pi says that these three treasures are those mentioned in
   Chapter 67. Underestimating one's enemy, one runs the risk of
   resorting to force; doing this is to 'lose the treasures' (see P. J.
   Lin 1977, 127).

70

a   Even though my words are easy to
understand and easy to put into
practice,
No one in the world really knows them or
lives by them.

b   My words have their origin, and my actions
receive their impetus, in the source of
all things.
If this is not understood, then I am not
understood.

c   Because so few understand my words, they
are prized so highly.
Therefore, the Sage appears wearing coarse
clothing, concealing the true treasure
in his heart.

71

a   To know that you do not know, this is best.
Not to know, whilst thinking that one does
know, this is to be flawed.
Recognising this defect as a defect
Is the way to be free of the defect.
The Sage is not flawed

Because he recognises the flaw as a flaw.

Therefore he is flawless.[1]

---

1   I follow Henricks (1990, 168) who remarks, 'Although *ping* [in this
     chapter] does mean "disease" ... here it is best translated, I feel,
     as "flaw" (or "fault" or "defect").'

72

a   Unless the people stand in awe of the
              authority over them,
         A greater authority will soon take over.[1]

b   Let them manage their own domestic affairs
              for themselves;
         Let them work according to their own
              dispositions.
         If you do not oppress them, they will not be
              oppressed.[2]

c   Therefore, the Sage knows himself
         But does not reveal himself.
         He respects himself
         Without being arrogant.
         Thus he discards one and chooses the other.

---

1   *or* The people may not stand in awe of their ruler's authority; But
     an authority greater than this [Heaven or Tao] will bring them to
     an end they deserve.
2   i.e. if the people are not oppressed, and are left to conduct their
     affairs for themselves, they will not resist or resent the authority
     of the state.

73

a   He who is courageous in taking action is
            soon killed.
      He who is courageous in remaining passive
            keeps his life.
      Of the two kinds of courage, one is harmful
            and the other is advantageous.
      Who knows why Heaven disapproves of one
            kind?
      Even the Sage is unsure how to answer this.

b   The Way of Heaven accomplishes without
            competing;
      Without declaring its will it receives a
            response;
      Without summoning, things come to it of
            their own accord;
      It accomplishes slowly, with well-laid plans.

c   The net of Heaven is vast,
      And though its mesh is very wide,
      Nothing can slip through.

74

a   If the people are not afraid to die,
     How can you threaten them with death?

b   If the people are kept in constant fear of
          death,
     And if it were possible to arrest and put to
          death the law-breakers,
     Who would dare do this?[1]

c   It is the master executioner[2] who does the
          killing.
     To assume the role of the master executioner
          and do the killing for oneself
     Is like carving wood for oneself
     Instead of leaving it to the master carpenter.
     Those who carve wood for themselves
     Instead of leaving it to the master carpenter
     Rarely escape without cutting their own
          hands.

---

1 There is an ambiguity here between 'Who would dare break the
   law?' and 'Who would dare put to death the law-breakers?' In the
   light of 74c, the latter interpretation seems to make more sense.
2 i.e. Heaven.

75

a   If the people go hungry
It is because the rulers take too much in
      taxes.
This is why they go hungry.

b   If the people prove difficult to rule
It is because the rulers interfere too much.[1]
This is why they prove difficult to rule.

c   If the people take death too lightly
It is because they are engrossed in seeking
      life's pleasures.
This is why the people take death too lightly.

d   It is only by ceasing to seek after life's
      pleasures that one will find life
      pleasurable.

1   i.e. they are trying to do too many things, and are not following the Taoist way of non-action.

76

a   When living, a man is supple and soft;
But dead, he is hard and stiff.
The myriad creatures, including grass and
      trees, when living, are pliant and frail;
But dead, they are withered and dry.

b   Therefore the hard and the stiff are disciples
      of death,
Whilst the supple and the soft are disciples of
      life.

c   An inflexible army cannot win.
A tree that cannot bend will break.

d   The hard and inflexible take the lower
      position.
The soft and weak take the higher position.[1]

1 i.e. hard and inflexible are inferior to soft and weak.

77

a   The Way of Heaven is like the drawing of a
      bow.
What is high is brought lower, and what is
      low is brought higher.[1]

What is too long is shortened;
What is too short is lengthened.[2]

b   The Way of Heaven is to take away from
            what is excessive
And to replenish what is deficient.
But the Way of Man is different:
It takes away from those who have little,
And gives to those who already have plenty.
Who is able to offer the world whatever he
            has in excess?
Only the man of Tao.

c   Therefore the Sage works without claiming
            reward,
Accomplishes without taking credit.
He has no desire to display his excellence.

1   i.e. when the string of a bow is drawn back, the top of the bow,
    as it bends, is pulled down (to some extent) and the bottom of
    the bow is pulled up. This simile is meant to illustrate the way
    Heaven makes things equal, and evens things out.
2   The simile is continued by referring to the string of the bow. If it is
    too long it must be shortened, and vice versa.

78

a   Under Heaven, nothing is softer and weaker
             than water.
     Yet nothing is better for attacking the hard
             and the strong.
     There is no better substitute.

b   All under Heaven know that the weak
             overcomes the strong
     And the soft overcomes the hard.
     Yet there are none who practise this.

c   Therefore the Sage says:
             He who takes upon himself the disgrace
                 of the country
             Is fit to be lord of the land.
             He who takes upon himself the
                 misfortunes of the country
             Is fit to be king of the empire.

d   True words seem paradoxical.

79

a   When a bad grudge is settled,
     Some enmity is bound to remain.
     How can this be considered acceptable?

b   Therefore the Sage keeps to his side of the
              contract
      But does not hold the other party to their
              promise.
      He who has Virtue will honour the contract,
      Whilst he who is without Virtue expects
              others to meet their obligations.
      It is the Way of Heaven to be impartial;
      It stays always with the good man.

80

a   The smaller the country, the fewer the
              people.[1]
      Even though they have machines that can
              do the work of ten, or a hundred
              men, they are never used.
      The people take death seriously, so do not
              travel far.[2]
      Even though they have boats and carriages,
              no one rides in them.
      Even though they have armour and weapons,
              no one displays them.

b   Let the people return to knotting cords.[3]
      Let them find their plain food sweet,
              their simple clothes fine,
              their modest dwellings secure;

And they would be happy with their
way of life.

c   Although the two peoples of the
neighbouring countries are so close
That they can see each other, and hear each
other's cocks crowing and dogs
barking,
They will leave each other alone and grow
old and die
Without ever having visited each other.

1 In this chapter, Lao Tzu describes an ideal society.
2 i.e. the more one travels, the more one risks accident and injury.
Besides, in an ideal society, affairs would be conducted in such a
way that need for travel becomes redundant.
3 historically, a practice prior to, and more simple than, writing.

81

a   True words are not beautiful;
Beautiful words are not true.
Those who are good do not argue;
Those who argue are not good.
Those who are wise are not learned;
Those who are learned are not wise.

b   The Sage does not store up possessions.
The more he helps others, the more he fulfils
himself.

The more he gives to others, the more he has
for himself.

c   The Way of Heaven is to benefit others
whilst harming no one.
The Way of the Sage is to accomplish
without striving.

GLOSSARY

(Numbers in brackets refer to chapters or sections of chapters in the *Tao Te Ching*. Cross-references within the Glossary are indicated by **bold type**.)

Chuang Tzu (*Chuang Chou*)

The *Chuang Tzu* (named after its supposed author) stands with the *Tao Te Ching* as one of the most important sources of Taoist philosophy. In style it is very different from the *Tao Te Ching*, being written (mostly) in continuous prose, its many different sections addressing distinct points or narrating fables which serve to illustrate specific ideas, some of which anticipate the style of later Zen writings.

The traditional view, now rejected by modern scholars, is that Chuang Tzu as a disciple of **Lao Tzu** carried on the tradition of the *Tao Te Ching*. This is almost certainly false. Even though the text of the *Chuang Tzu* as we have it today was restructured, added to, and commentaries inserted by editors and commentators in ancient times, there is reason to believe that a coherent core text, perhaps written by Chuang Chou, was in circulation by the latter half of the fourth century BC – earlier than the *Tao Te Ching* which is unattested until about 250 BC.

Modern scholars are agreed that the core text, the first seven chapters of the *Chuang Tzu* which demonstrate a unity of style and coherence of exposition, were written by Chuang Chou some time around 320 BC.

Over the next two centuries, editors and commentators working in the tradition which Chuang Chou inaugurated collected into the *Chuang Tzu* a range of similar and related texts. Some scholars believe that some odd fragments consigned to the 'Mixed Chapters' may be from the hand of Chuang Chou (see Graham 1989, 173).

The *Chuang Tzu* and the *Tao Te Ching* were not at first associated. In the text named after its author Hsün Tzu (*c*.313–238 BC), the *Chuang Tzu* and the *Tao Te Ching* are mentioned in separate lists of the philosophers. In the final chapter of the *Chuang Tzu* itself – Chapter 33 (second century BC) – Lao Tzu and Chuang Chou are presented as belonging to separate schools. The notion of a distinct 'Taoist school', the *tao chia*, did not appear until Ssu-ma T'an (died 110 BC) made his classification of the 'Six Schools'.

The *Chuang Tzu* teaches a distinct doctrine of freedom. The person who can free themselves from conventional standards of behaviour, thinking, relations with others, well-being and so on, will be incapable of suffering harm and misfortune, since what is harmful is established by convention. The *Chuang Tzu* is contemptuous of civilised life in a variety of ways, seeing civilisation not as a source of better and comfortable living to be praised and encouraged, but as a source of perverted and artificial living, to be condemned and rejected.

In content, in the most general of senses, Lao Tzu is concerned with statecraft, and his text is addressed to the ruler. Chuang Chou is concerned with personal salvation, and his text is addressed to the individual.

In style the *Chuang Tzu* is very different from the *Tao Te Ching*, employing philosophical expositions, dialogues, tales and fables – in contrast to the *Tao Te Ching's* pithy and precise aphorisms. In tone, the *Chuang Tzu* is often light-hearted (though with serious intent), even frivolous. The *Tao Te Ching* rejects convention, the *Chuang Tzu* ridicules it; the *Tao Te Ching* warns against display of wealth and rank, the *Chuang Tzu* condemns it. Lao Tzu is serious, if not stern; Chuang Chou is affable, if not sanguine. Not that the *Chuang Tzu* is transparent and its philosophy obvious. In ridiculing conventional wisdom as well as the processes of rational discourse itself, Chuang Chou is aware that he has removed the ground on which he needs to build his own arguments. This perhaps doesn't matter, since the *Chuang Tzu* aims to set its student on a path towards insight, not merely to win a philosophical debate. In this light Chuang Chou's character Chang Wu Tzu's saying 'I'm going to try speaking some reckless words and I want you to listen to them recklessly' (*Chuang Tzu* Chapter 2, trans. Watson 1968, 47) begins to make sense.

Confucius (*K'ung Fu Tzu*: 551–479 BC)

The most famous of Chinese philosophers, whose school of Confucianism (*ju-chia*: 'School of Scholars') has influenced Chinese society more than any other. His teachings are found in the *Analects* (*Lun-yü*; see Lau 1979), an extensive collection of sayings and dialogues probably compiled some time after Confucius' death by a second generation of disciples. His doctrines were developed and promoted by Mencius (*Meng Tzu*: c.372–289 BC) and Hsün Tzu (c.313–238 BC).

Confucius set himself the task of saving society from disorder and decline. He looked back nostalgically to an earlier, golden age at the dawn of the Chou Dynasty, when Confucius' hero, the Duke of Chou, ruled a society adhering to strict cultural values and social norms, transmitted and inculcated by a whole array of complex ritual observances. So long as the rituals were faithfully followed, the ruler would continue to enjoy the mandate of Heaven, and the state would continue to enjoy peace, harmony and prosperity.

Two centuries before Confucius, the Chou kings lost political power to a group of feudal lords; Confucius and others would maintain that this breakdown in cultural continuity resulted in the mandate of Heaven being withdrawn, and as a consequence, social and moral decline set in.

To save society from this decline and re-establish the mandate of Heaven, Confucius sought to re-introduce a strict system of social conduct revolving around rigid ritual practices. His aim was to restore the purity of the traditional institutions of the family, the community and the state, by constraining all social interactions within pre-set systems of rules and rituals.

Lao Tzu and **Chuang Tzu** (and others belonging to the school of philosophical Taoism: *tao chia*) agree with

Confucius that human beings are intrinsically morally good, and become bad, if they do, only because they are corrupted by individuals and institutions already corrupted. But the Taoists disagree with Confucius over the imposing of rigid **rules** and ritual practices. Taoists believe that, far from promoting harmony and order in society, rules are a positive hindrance. Lao Tzu, in Chapter 38 of the *Tao Te Ching* remarks that 'Merely following rules is a pretence of trust and loyalty, and is the beginning of confusion.' Indeed, 'when Tao is lost, goodness remains' (also Chapter 38). For if people were conducting their affairs motivated only by the natural goodness Tao had nurtured in them, there would be no need for Confucius' rules and rituals. To the extent that rules and rituals appear to be needed, people's natural goodness has already been undermined by the corrupting influences of institutions and individuals. This corruption of natural goodness would cease were the ruler to see to it that the institutions by which society is run carried out their roles according to Taoist morality; indeed, in a Taoist society, many of the institutions previously thought so indispensable could be abandoned.

In a Confucian society, the people are not being guided by their own natural goodness, but are being coerced and confined by rules and regulations. In such a society, if someone performs some duty for me, how can I tell whether they are acting out of fear of punishment should they fail in their performance, or out of a genuine desire to act well? Put bluntly, Confucius seeks to paste a pleasing veneer over what is already corrupt and set contrary to the Tao. In the ideal Taoist society, the question of trying to be good doesn't even arise, for the people, holding to Tao, are naturally good even without thinking about it. One only needs to think about doing good if one is aware of the possibility of choosing the bad option. One may be good spontaneously and naturally – the Taoist ideal – or one may be good by being aware that one is rejecting the bad. Even in rejecting the bad, the bad must have presented itself as a possibility. When one is aware that there is a choice between the good and the bad, evil has already been admitted to the world (see *Tao Te Ching* Chapter 2).

Heaven and Earth (*t'ien ti*)

T'ien ti designates the universe as a whole. In ancient Chinese philosophy, Heaven and Earth interact with each other, and in doing so produce the phenomenal world (the world as it seems to us). Heaven is conceived of as active, and it acts upon the passive Earth. Heaven is masculine, and Earth feminine. In terms of **yin and yang**, Earth is yin, and Heaven is yang. 'Heaven' frequently means, simply, 'nature' or 'the natural order'. When ancient Chinese philosophy says that all things happen in accord with Heaven, or at Heaven's beckoning, this means essentially what modern-day scientists mean when they say that everything happens in accord with the laws of nature. Heaven is seen as the controlling, activating force responsible for everything that happens. Thought of in this way, 'Heaven' appears to be essentially the same as **Tao**.

Keeping to, holding to, following the Tao

Someone who 'holds to the **Tao**' perceives matters along the lines of **Lao Tzu**, in agreement with the principles (metaphysical and ethical) expressed in the *Tao Te Ching*. Holding to the Tao is like staying on a highway, knowing where one is going, and not being distracted into turning off down a side-road where one will lose one's way. (See *Tao Te Ching* Chapter 53.)

Knowledge (*chih*)

The *Tao Te Ching* is hostile to knowledge, and goes so far as to tell us to 'abandon knowledge' (19a). Knowledge, says the Taoist, is potentially harmful.

Sometimes the *Tao Te Ching* means to refer in particular to knowledge of Confucian rites. (See the Glossary entry for **Confucius.**) Taoists maintain that if society can function only if **rules** and rigid codes of practice are adopted, then something seriously wrong has already occurred: specifically, people have already fallen from their state of natural goodness into a state where they are corrupted by desires, competition, jealousies and selfishness.

> Give up scheming and abandon gain,
> And robbers and thieves will disappear (19a).

Benevolence (*jen*) and morality (*i*) are two key concepts in Confucian thought. The Taoist laughs at the idea that you can make people act benevolently and morally by imposing rules and codes of practice. If people are not benevolent and moral, no amount of enforced rule-directed behaviour is going to make any difference.

Sometimes the *Tao Te Ching* means to refer to knowledge in a more general sense. 'Knowledge leads to desire, which leads to action, which disturbs the peace of society' (Chen 1989, 60). When the *Tao Te Ching* says that the people are ruled wisely when the ruler 'empties their hearts and fills their bellies,' we should understand this to mean that people's hearts (minds) are emptied of knowledge. Without knowledge, and the desires that knowledge kindles, people cannot pursue 'unnatural' goals. By 'filling their bellies' the wise ruler makes provision for people to obtain what they really need: food, shelter and clothing.

Non-action (*wu wei*)

Literally: 'without action'. (See the discussion of *wu wei* in the Introduction.)

Taoists model their thoughts and actions on the Tao itself, and thereby do not intervene or interfere with the natural course of events. Taking this stance, all things are allowed to develop in accord with their own natures.

The person who manages their affairs *wu wei* responds to events spontaneously and without being motivated by thoughts of loss or gain, success or failure. They do what is necessary to live at peace and in harmony with their environment and with their neighbours. They do not form intentions or have an eye on any particular goal, and respond unthinkingly (but not inappropriately) to events as they un-fold.

To act *wu wei* you should act without placing any store on the outcome, abandon all thought of satisfying desires, and – at least in some circumstances – consider whether any *action* is really required at all. Do not let pressures placed on you by others direct your actions – after all, the tree is not pressured into swaying in the breeze and the rain is not pressured to fall, and on your part, you must not force events in directions they are not naturally inclined to follow. Take care of events without taking charge of them.

Lao Tzu (*Lao Tan*)

Traditionally, Lao Tzu is the author of the *Tao Te Ching*, and a contemporary of **Confucius** (sixth century BC). It is doubtful that Lao Tzu ever existed (certainly in the sixth century BC), and it is probable that the *Tao Te Ching* is really an anthology which was compiled in the third century BC by several, un-known authors. 'Lao Tzu' means 'old master' (in the sense of 'teacher'). The traditional story of Lao Tzu (in the *Shih Chi*) tells that he was named Lao Tan and worked as court archi-vist in the state of Chou, but seeing the state fall into moral decline, decided to leave the country, and travelled west-wards. At the border, the 'Keeper of the Pass' asked him to write a book embodying the wisdom he had learned, and the *Tao Te Ching* was the result. Other stories claim, preposter-ously, that he went to India and taught the Buddha, or in-deed that he and the Buddha are the same person.

Religious Taoism (*tao chiao*)

Religious **Taoism** is a mixture of superstition and magic, al-chemy and the quest for immortality. Followers may be found in Taiwan, Hong Kong, and other far-eastern locations. This strand of Taoism post-dates Philosophical Taoism (*tao chia*) by several centuries. It appears to have corrupted and debased the significantly earlier and sophisticated outlook of Philosophical Taoism. The quest for immortality appears to be particularly at odds with the practice of *wu wei* (**non-action**), and with the overall thrust of Philosophical Taoism in general, which urges the student to abandon ambitious schemes and projects (especially self-interested ones) and to embrace the natural flow and development of events, including the facts of human ageing, illness, and eventual dying. Death is conceived of as '**returning** to the source', and in this sense is better thought of as a complete and thoroughgoing transformation rather than the literal end.

Returning (*fu* or *fan*)

All things in the phenomenal world (the world as it seems to us) are subject to the principle of *fu*, 'return', or *fan*, 'reversion'. At that moment when a process that something is undergoing reaches an extreme, or has proceeded to a point where no further development is possible, a 'reversion' or 'return' occurs. At this point, the process starts again from the beginning, or proceeds in reverse as it were, back towards the starting position.

The interaction of **yin and yang** is conceived of in much the same way. Not only do the polar energies of yin and yang interact to give rise to the phenomenal world, but each energy is continuously in the process of transforming into its opposite. This is symbolised in the yin-yang symbol: the two spots show that the two energies are about to transform themselves each into their opposite.

Indeed, the **Tao** itself is subject to this principle: 'The motion of the Tao is to return' (40a); 'Being great is to go ever-onward. Going ever-onward is to reach everywhere. Reaching everywhere is to return' (25b).

The principle of returning is readily apparent in the world of natural phenomena. A tree, for instance, will steadily grow until it is mature. But having reached this extreme, because it is so tall, it is vulnerable (to an extent that it was not before) to high winds, and so cannot stand indefinitely, but will be blown down in the next high wind. In the beginning, this tree grew from a seed, and of course, throughout its life it has produced and shed an untold number of seeds, and some of these will have germinated, taken root and started to grow up as new saplings. This cyclical process of generation, growth and destruction goes on indefinitely. Astronomers have discovered that stars are formed from the condensation of interstellar dust and gas. Under the pull of gravity more and more dust and gas is drawn in until the press of material is so high that nuclear reactions occur and the star bursts into life. Many millions of years later, when all its nuclear material has been consumed, the star will blow apart as a supernova scattering dust and gas into the interstellar void, and the whole process will be repeated.

All things in existence, says the Taoist, are governed by such cyclical processes.

Rules

The *Tao Te Ching* is very much against rules.

Human beings are naturally disposed to behave in certain ways. So, very generally, either rules are framed which accord with these natural dispositions, and so are never broken, or rules are framed which are *not* in accord with these natural dispositions. Either way, the rules serve no purpose.

When the natural order has been corrupted or abandoned to such an extent that people begin to behave badly, how can the attempt to enforce laws improve the situation? Some people drink and drive (for instance) despite the rules prohibiting such anti-social behaviour. The problem can be solved only by encouraging people to lead more rewarding lives, doing away with the need to drink too much in the first place.

(See also **Confucius** and **Knowledge**.)

Sage (*sheng jen*)

The Taoist Sage models his or her thoughts and actions on the Tao itself. They are *wu chih*, without knowledge, *wu yü*, without desire, and they accomplish their tasks *wu wei*, without acting. The Sage loves tranquillity (57c), does not compete (22b, 66d), and does not reveal himself (72c). The Sage never strives to attain anything, so never fails; never tries to hold onto anything, so never loses. The Sage describes their outlook like this: 'Mysteriously, wonderfully, I bid farewell to what goes, I greet what comes; for what comes cannot be denied, and what goes cannot be detained.' (*Chuang Tzu*, Chapter 20: Watson 1968, 213)

Superior Man (*chün tsu*)

For Confucius the *chün tsu*, the 'lord's son', often translated as 'superior man', is the exemplary person possessing moral rectitude (see Hall & Ames, 1987 176–82 and 188–92), but the phrase *chün tsu* does not actually appear in the *Tao Te Ching*. In those places where I have put 'superior man' (8, 38e, 41a) other translators favour a variety of essentially synonymous expressions: 'best man', 'man of supreme goodness', 'full-grown man', 'Great Man', 'truly great man', 'superior scholar', 'highest type of man', 'wise student', 'truly cultivated man', 'man of large mind', 'noble man', and indeed sometimes, 'superior man'. Occasionally some translators employ **'sage'**. The *Tao Te Ching* in 38e employs *ta chang fu*, 'truly great man', and in 41a employs the phrase *sheng shih*, 'superior scholar'.

Some translators for Chapter 8 have simply 'best', in the abstract; occasionally they mean to refer to the Tao. The *Tao Te Ching* has *shang shan*, 'superior goodness', or simply 'best'.

I interpret this to mean the best man, the one possessing 'superior goodness'. Wing-tsit Chan remarks that **Wang Pi** took the phrase 'best' to mean 'the best man'. Rump and Chan (1979, 26) remark that they follow Wang Pi, 'not only because his commentary on the text is the oldest and most reliable, but also because the *Lao Tzu* deals with man's way of life more than abstract ideas.'

Tao

(See the longer exposition in the Introduction.) This is the central concept in the *Tao Te Ching*. For Taoists following **Lao Tzu** and **Chuang Tzu**, Tao is the source of being which all things in the universe enjoy; they arise from it, are sustained and nurtured by it until, in the end, they **'return'** to it (i.e. cease to exist).

In so far as the Tao is that which gives being to things, it is itself not a thing. Tao is non-being, which is the mother of being, which produces all things. It is nameless, for it is greater than anything that can be named. It takes no action. It leaves things alone. It supports all things, but does not take possession of them. It lets things transform themselves. It does nothing, yet all things are thereby accomplished.

The Tao is eternal, spontaneous, nameless and indescribable, at once the beginning of all things and the way in which they pursue their course. It is non-being in the sense of not being any particular thing.

No particular conception, of course, amounts to conceiving of the Tao in its totality or 'as it really is', and neither do all the different conceptions taken as a cumulative whole constitute a total conception. To conceive of the Tao in a complete way is not something that the human intellect can logically do, hence 'The Tao that can be put in words is not the ever-abiding Tao' (1a).

The original meaning of the Chinese character 'tao' is 'path', in the sense of a 'way that is followed'. Hence by extension, 'tao' also means 'the way something is done', 'practice', 'procedure', 'method', and even 'principle'. The metaphysical entity denoted by 'Tao' can be thought of as 'the way in which the universe is manifested'.

Taoism

The term in English is somewhat misleading, as it is used to refer both to *tao chia* (Philosophical Taoism) and to *tao chiao* (**Religious Taoism**). The treatment of **Lao Tzu's** *Tao Te Ching* in this book remains strictly confined to Philosophical Taoism, whose followers emphasised the importance of modelling one's values and actions on the **Tao** itself. Religious Taoism is a later, eclectic, movement, whose followers' main aim is the attainment of immortality through special practices, including physical exercise, breathing techniques, alchemical and sexual practices.

Te *see* Virtue

Ten Thousand Things (*wan-wu*)

Wan wu means, literally, 'ten thousand things', meaning 'all things', 'all creation', 'innumerable', 'everything'. It is a conventional expression denoting everything that there is in the universe. Some translators use expressions such as 'ten thousand creatures' and 'myriad creatures' (cf. Lau 1963), emphasising the natural world over inanimate things.

Uncarved Block (*p'u*)

The concept of the uncarved block is one of the Taoist symbols for simplicity. It offers an image of the natural state of human beings, and their societies, before contaminating influences set in, and before individuals are affected by the cultures in which they grow up, after which people, in varying degrees fall prey to desires for 'non-Taoist' ends, such as wealth, status and power. The *Tao Te Ching* teaches that to return to the primordial state of *p'u*, the uncarved block, we must give up our desires and attachments, because what we have been pursuing in error really has no value, and further, is actually the cause of all our troubles.

Under Heaven / Beneath Heaven (*t'ien hsia*)

The phrase denotes the phenomenal world, the world of ordinary experience. We all live 'under Heaven', and anything we do, any task attempted, takes place 'under Heaven'. The expression 'all under Heaven', which occurs in the *Tao Te Ching*, means, simply, 'everyone'. In various contexts, as Chen (1989, 127) points out, *t'ien hsia* 'can be taken to mean the natural world, the natural environment, or the state, the empire.'

Virtue (*te*)

With regard to any particular thing, *te* is that enabling power which gives this thing that agglomeration of characteristics and capacities which make it the thing that it is, rather than something else. If we ask 'In virtue of *what* is this thing this thing?' or 'In virtue of *what* does this thing flourish in the way that it does?' the answer is *te*. *Te* is that which each thing receives from the **Tao** by which it manifests in the phenomenal world (the world as it seems to us). Thus Tao is the source of all things, and *te* is the means by which they are generated.

The person who enjoys perfect *te* will thereby be a fully virtuous person in the moral sense. In giving up **knowledge**, in not contending, in responding to circumstance spontaneously, the **Sage** transforms into a more virtuous person in the moral sense, but also is thereby conceived as increasing his *te* (54b), or accumulating *te* (59a) simply because he is approaching closer to the natural ideal of what a human being really is.

Wang Pi (AD 226-249)

The oldest extant commentary on the *Tao Te Ching* was written by Wang Pi. His is the most philosophical of commentaries on this text, raising the understanding of Taoism to the metaphysical level. 'It is not an exaggeration to say that Chinese metaphysics began with Wang's commentary on the *Lao Tzu*.' (Rump and Chan 1979, ix.) Many current translations of the *Tao Te Ching* are based on Wang Pi's edition. In 1973 in south-central China near Chang Sha (Hunan Province) in the village of Ma Wang Tui, amongst a wide range of texts, two copies of the *Tao Te Ching* written on silk, were discovered. The Ma Wang Tui manuscripts of the *Tao Te Ching* are the oldest known versions. They are sometimes referred to as the *Te Tao Ching* because in these editions Chapters 38-81 (commencing with the character *te*) come before Chapters 1-37 (commencing with the character *tao*). The Ma Wang Tui manuscripts are translated by Henricks (1990) and by Lau (1982). The differences between the Ma Wang Tui texts and the Wang Pi text are pretty much of interest only to scholars: 'The Ma-wang-tui texts do not differ in any *radical* way from later versions of the text' (Henricks 1990, xv).

Wu-wei *see* non-action

Yin and Yang

Yin and *yang* are mentioned just once in the *Tao Te Ching* (42b). Scholars generally agree that these terms originally referred to the 'sunless' and the 'sunny'. Thus, for instance, the south side of a hill is *yang* and the north side is *yin*. Generally, *yang* is strong and active, whilst *yin* is weak and passive. The principles and forces of nature fall readily into the two categories. Hard is *yang*, soft is *yin*. Dry, hot, big, full, are *yang*. Wet, cold, small, empty, are *yin*.

In Chinese philosophy generally, neither *yin* nor *yang* is superior to the other. Strong is not better than weak, and female is not inferior to male. With respect to all these 'opposites' each requires its counterpart, or neither would exist. There is no male without female, no shade without light; whatever is small is so only by comparison to the large, whatever comes last can only do so in contrast to what comes first.

Though, interestingly, when discussing strategies for survival (for both the individual in society and for the ruler of the state), the *Tao Te Ching* often favours the *yin*-like opposite: *wu wei* (not acting) is better than *wei* (acting) and *wu yü* (without desire) is preferred to *yü* (desire). Nothing, rather than something, is praised: it is the vacant space at the centre of a wheel, inside a vessel and between and through the walls of a room that make these things usable (11).

The *Tao Te Ching* emphasises the cycles in nature whereby things that have been strong, hard, straight, etc. eventually revert to their opposite, becoming weak, soft, bent, etc. Trying to maintain one extreme is not possible: 'The finely honed blade will soon lose its sharpness' (9b).

(See **Returning**.)

BIBLIOGRAPHY

Works marked * contain complete translations of the *Tao Te Ching*. Works marked † contain abridged translations, or a selection of chapters from the *Tao Te Ching*.

* Addiss, Stephen and Stanley Lombardo. 1993. *Lao-tzu: Tao Te Ching*. Indianapolis: Hackett.

Allinson, Robert E. 1989. *Chuang-Tzu for Spiritual Transformation: An Analysis of the Inner Chapers*. Albany, NY: State University of New York Press.

* Ames, Roger T. and David L. Hall. 2003. *Daodejing "Making this Life Significant": A Philosophical Translation*. New York: Ballantine Books.

Billington, Ray. 1990. *East of Existentialism: The Tao of the West*. London: Unwin Hyman.

* Carus, Paul. 1898. *Lao-tze's Tao-Teh-King*. Chicago: Open Court.

* ———— and D. T. Suzuki. 1913 [1974]. *The Canon of Reason and Virtue (Lao-Tzu's Tao The King)*. La Salle: Open Court.

Chan, Alan K. L. 1991. *Two Visions of the Way: A Study of the Wang Pi and the Ho-shang Kung Commentaries on the* Lao-Tzu. Albany, NY: State University of New York Press.

Chan, Wing-tsit. 1967a. Chinese philosophy, in Edwards 1967.

————. 1967b. Confucius, in Edwards 1967.

————. 1967c. Chuang Tzu, in Edwards 1967.

————. 1967d. Lao Tzu, in Edwards 1967.

* ————. 1969. *A Source Book in Chinese Philosophy*. Princeton, NJ: Princeton University Press.

Chang Chung-yuan. 1963. *Creativity and Taoism*. New York: Harper & Row.

* Chen, Ellen M. 1989. *The Tao Te Ching: A New Translation with Commentary*. New York: Paragon House.

* Cheng, Man-jan. 1981. *Lao-Tzu: 'My Words Are Very Easy to Understand'*. trans. Tam C. Gibbs. Richmond, CA: North Atlantic Books.

* Ch'en Ku-ying. 1977. *Lao Tzu: Text, Notes, and Commentary*. trans. Rhett Y. W. Young and Roger T. Ames. San Francisco: Chinese Materials Centre.

* Ch'u Ta-Kao. 1959 [1985]. *Tao Tê Ching*. London: Mandala Books.

Cleary, T. 1986. *The Taoist I Ching*. Boston: Shambhala.

———. 1988. *Awakening to the Tao* (Liu I-ming). Boston: Shambhala.

———. 1991. *Wen-tzu: Understanding the Mysteries* (Lao-tzu). Boston: Shambhala.

———. 1992a. *The Essential Confucius*. New York: Harper-Collins.

* ———. 1992b. *The Essential Tao*. New York: HarperCollins.

Cooper, J. C. 1981. *Yin & Yang: The Taoist Harmony of Opposites*. Wellingborough: Aquarian Press.

———. 1990. *Taoism: the Way of the Mystic*. Wellingborough: Aquarian Press.

Creel, H. G. 1982. *What is Taoism?* Chicago: University of Chicago Press.

* Dalton, Jerry O. 1994. *Backward Down the Path: A New Approach to the Tao Te Ching*. Atlanta: Humanics New Age.

Daoren, Huanchu. 1990. *Back to Beginnings: Reflections on the Tao*. trans. Thomas Cleary. Boston: Shambhala.

Dawson, R. 1981. *Confucius*. Oxford: Oxford University Press.

———. 1984. *A New Introduction to Classical Chinese*. Oxford: Clardendon Press.

Dreher, Diane. 1990. *The Tao of Peace*. London: Mandala.

* Duyvendak, J. J. L. 1954 [1992]. *Tao Te Ching: The Book of the Way and Its Virtue*. London: John Murray.

Eichhorn, W. 1977. Taoism, in Zaehner 1977.

Edwards, P. ed. 1967. *The Encyclopedia of Philosophy*. New York: Macmillan.

* Feng, Gia-Fu and J. English. 1973. *Lao Tsu: Tao Te Ching*. London: Wildwood House.

———. 1974. *Chuang Tsu: Inner Chapters*. New York: Vintage Books.

* Freke, Timothy. 1995. *Lao Tzu's Tao Te Ching*. London: Piatkus.

† Fung Yu-lan. 1983. *A History of Chinese Philosophy*. Vol. 1. trans. Derk Bodde. Princeton, NJ: Princeton University Press.

Giles, Herbert A. 1926. *Chuang Tzŭ: Taoist Philosopher and Chinese Mystic*. 2nd ed. London: George Allen & Unwin.

Graham, A. C. 1981. *Chuang-Tzŭ: The Inner Chapters*. London: George Allen & Unwin.

———. 1986. *Studies in Chinese Philosophy and Philosophical Literature*. Albany, NY: State University of New York Press.

———. 1989. *Disputers of the Tao*. La Salle: Open Court.

———. 1990. *The Book of Lieh-tzŭ*. New York: Columbia University Press.

———. 1992. *Unreason Within Reason: Essays on the Outskirts of Rationality*. La Salle: Open Court.

* Grigg, Ray. 1995. *The New Lao Tzu: A Comtemporary Tao Te Ching*. Boston, Rutland & Tokyo: Tuttle.

* Henricks, Robert G. 1990. *Lao-Tzu: Te-Tao Ching*. London: Bodley Head.

Herbert, Edward. 1951 [1992]. *A Confucian Notebook*. London: John Murray.

Hinnells, J. R. ed. 1984. *Dictionary of Religions*. Harmondsworth: Penguin.

† Hoff, Benjamin. 1981. *The Way to Life*. New York & Tokyo: John Weatherhill.

———. 1982. *The Tao of Pooh*. London: Methuen.

———. 1992. *The Te of Piglet*. London: Methuen.

† Hughes, E. R. 1942. *Chinese Philosophy in Classical Times*. London: Dent.

Ivanhoe, Philip J. 2000. *Confucian Moral Self Cultivation*. 2nd ed. Indianapolis: Hackett.

* ———. 2002. *The Daodejing of Laozi.* New York: Seven Bridges Press.
* Jiyu, Ren. 1993. *The Book of Lao Zi.* Beijing: Foreign Languages Press.
† Kaltenmark, M. 1969. *Lao Tzu and Taoism.* trans. Roger Greaves. Stanford, CA: Stanford University Press.
* Karlgren, Bernhard. 1975. *Notes on Lao Tse.* reprinted from The Museum of Far Eastern Antiquities: Bulletin No. 47, Stockholm.
Kjellberg, Paul and Philip J. Ivanhoe, eds. 1996. *Essays on Skepticism, Relativism, and Ethics in the Zhuangzi.* Albany, NY: State University Press of New York.
* Kwok, Man-ho, Martin Palmer, Jay Ramsay. 1993. *Tao Te Ching: A New Translation.* Shaftesbury: Element.
* Lao Tzu. 1983. *Tao Te Ching.* trans. anon. Santa Barbara: Concord Grove Press.
* LaFargue, Michael. 1994. *Tao and Method: A Reasoned Approach to the Tao Te Ching.* Albany, NY: State University of New York Press.
Lau, D. C. 1963. *Lao Tzu: Tao Te Ching.* London: Penguin.
——— 1979. *The Analects* (Confucius). Harmondsworth: Penguin.
* ———. 1982. *Tao Te Ching.* Hong Kong: Chinese University Press.
* Legge, J. 1891 [1962]. *The Texts of Taoism.* 2 vols. New York: Dover.
* Lin, P. J. 1977. *A Translation of Lao Tzu's Tao Te Ching and Wang Pi's Commentary.* Ann Arbor: Center for Chinese Studies, University of Michigan.
Lin Yutang. 1938. *The Importance of Living.* London: Heinemann.
* ———. 1958. *The Wisdom of Laotse.* New York: Random House.
Loy Ching-yuen. 1990. *The Book of the Heart: Embracing the Tao.* trans. Trevor Cardan and Bella Chen. Boston & London: Shambhala.

Mair, Victor H. ed. 1983. *Experimental Essays on Chuang-tzu*. Hawaii: Asian Studies at Hawaii, No. 29. University of Hawaii Press.

* ———. 1990. *Tao Te Ching: The Classic Book of Integrity and the Way*. New York: Bantam Books.

* Maurer, H. 1986. *Tao: The Way of the Ways*. Aldershot: Wildwood House.

* Mears, I. 1922. *Tao Teh King by Lao Tzu*. London: Theosophical Publishing House.

Merton, Thomas. 1965 [1969]. *The Way of Chuang Tzu*. New York: New Directions.

* Metz, Pamela K. 1994. *The Tao of Learning: Lao Tzu's Tao Te Ching Adapted for a New Age*. Atlanta: Humanics New Age.

* Miles, Thomas H. 1992. *Tao Te Ching, Lao Tzu: About the Way of Nature and Its Powers*. New York: Avery Publishing.

* Mitchell, Stephen. 1988. *The Tao Te Ching of Lao Tzu*. London: Macmillan.

Morgan, Evan. 1974. *Tao The Great Luminant: Essays from the Huai Nan Tzu*. Taipei: Ch'eng Wen Publishing Co.

* Ni, Hua-Ching. 1979. *The Complete Works of Lao Tzu*. Malibu, CA: The Shrine of the Eternal Breath of Tao.

Palmer, Martin. 1996. *The Book of Chuang Tzu*. London: Penguin.

* Roberts, Moss. 2001. *Dao De Jing: The Book of the Way*. Berkeley: University of California Press.

Roth, Harold D. 1991. Psychology and self-cultivation in early Taoist thought. *Harvard Journal of Asiatic Studies* 51: 599–650.

* Rump, Ariane and Wing-tsit Chan. 1979. *Commentary on the Lao Tzu by Wang Pi*. Honolulu: University of Hawaii Press.

Schuhmacher, Stephan and Gert Woerner. 1989. *The Rider Encyclopedia of Eastern Philosophy and Religion*. London: Rider.

* Shaman Flowing Hands. 1992. *Lao Tzu: Dao Te King*. Penzance: Daoist Foundation.

Siklós, B. 1988. Philosophical and religious Taoism, in Sutherland 1988.

Smart, N. 1971. *The Religious Experience of Mankind*. London: Fontana.

† Smith, D. Howard. 1980. *The Wisdom of the Taoist Masters*. London: Sheldon Press.

Smullyan, Raymond M. 1977. *The Tao is Silent*. New York: Harper & Row.

* Star, Jonathan. 2001. *Tao Te Ching: The Definitive Edition*: New York: Tarcher/Putnam.

Sutherland, S. ed. 1988. *The World's Religions*. London: Routledge.

† Tsai Chih Chung. 1989. *The Sayings of Lao Zi*. trans. Koh Kok Kiang and Wong Lit Khiong. Singapore: Asiapac Books.

† ———. 1992. *The Sayings of Lao Zi: Book 2*. trans. Koh Kok Kiang. Singapore: Asiapac Books.

———. 1992. *Zhuangzi Speaks: The Music of Nature*. trans. Brian Bruya. Princeton, NJ: Princeton University Press.

* Waley, A. 1934 [1977]. *The Way and its Power*. London: Unwin.

———. 1939 [1982]. *Three Ways of Thought in Ancient China*. Stanford, CA: Stanford University Press.

Watson, Burton. 1964. *Chuang Tzu: Basic Writings*. New York: Columbia University Press. [Contains the seven 'Inner Chapters' plus Chapters 17, 18, 19 and 26.]

———. 1968. *The Complete Works of Chuang Tzu*. New York: Columbia University Press.

Watts, Alan. 1975 [1992]. *Tao: The Watercourse Way*. London: Arkana.

Welch, Holmes. 1966. *Taoism: The Parting of the Way*. Boston: Beacon Press.

Wieger, Léon. 1927 [1965]. *Chinese Characters*. New York: Dover.

* ———. 1984. *Wisdom of the Daoist Masters*. trans. Derek Bryce. Lampeter: Llanerch Enterprises.

† ———. 1988. *Philosophy and Religion in China*. trans. Derek Bryce. Lampeter: Llanerch Enterprises.

* ———. 1991. *Lao-Tzu: Tao-Te-Ching*. trans. Derek Bryce. Felinfach: Llanerch Publishers.

———. 1992. *Lieh-tzu*. trans. Derek Bryce. Felinfach: Llanerch Publishers.

* Wilhelm, Richard. 1985. *Tao Te Ching: The Book of Meaning*. trans. H. G. Ostwald. London: Arkana.

* Wing, R. L. 1986. *The Tao of Power*. Wellingborough: Aquarian Press.

* Wu, John C. H. 1989. *Lao Tzu: Tao Teh Ching*. Boston & Shaftesbury: Shambhala.

Wu, Kuang-ming. 1982. *Chuang Tzu: World Philosopher at Play*. New York & Chico: Crossroad and Scholars Press.

———. 1990. *The Butterfly as Companion: Meditations on the First Three Chapters of the Chuang Tzu*. Albany, NY: State University of New York Press.

* Wu, Yi. 1989. *The Book of Lao Tzu (the Tao Te Ching)*. San Francisco: Great Learning Publishing.

Zaehner, R. C. ed. 1977. *The Concise Encyclopedia of Living Faiths*. London: Hutchinson.

INDEX TO THE TAO TE CHING

Lao Tzu: Tao Te Ching
A New Version, with Introduction, Notes, Glossary and Index
Keith Seddon
First published in paperback by Lulu 2006
Published in hardback by Keith Seddon at Lulu 2008
© 2006, 2008 Keith Seddon

ISBN 978–0–955–68443–2 (hardback)
ISBN 978–1–847–28263–7 (paperback)

The illustrations in this book are taken from *The Mustard Seed Garden Manual of Painting*, Princeton University Press, 1977, certified by the publisher in 1995 as being in the public domain.

The main text of this book is set in Book Antiqua 10 & 11 pt. with Arial 10 and 12 pt. for display, and for all supplemental texts.